# A POSITIVE MANIFESTO

## How Appreciative Schools Can Transform Public Education

Leonard C. Burrello, Linda M. Beitz, and John L. Mann

ELEPHANT
ROCK
BOOKS

**ELEPHANT ROCK BOOKS**

Imprint of Elephant Rock Productions

Elephant Rock, PO Box 119, Ashford, CT 06278, U.S.A.

Elephant Rock Books are distributed by Small Press United,

a division of Independent Publishers Group.

10 9 8 7 6 5 4 3 2 1

ISBN: 978-0-9968649-0-9

Printed in the United States of America

Book Designed by Amanda Schwarz

Fisheye Graphic Services, Chicago

*For Dena, Debbie, Ramzi, and Jana*

# TABLE OF CONTENTS

# FOREWORD
## Positive Narratives:
## Appreciative Organizing in Public Education

## THE PERFECT STORM IN WARREN TOWNSHIP

In 2009 a series of disruptive events created temporary chaos in this Indiana school district. First, a 3.5-million-dollar cut in state support hit Warren's bottom line as the district struggled to make technology upgrades to its older elementary schools. Plus, data revealed a serious demographic and racial disparity between schools. Finally, middle school enrollments were dropping.

What options were open to district leadership within this complex set of forces? They could close a number of schools and spend the savings on tutors and enrichment programs. In other words, do what had been done in the past, and carry on with what was left. Or was there another pathway to equity and opportunity for all?

Warren's new assistant superintendent of elementary schools, Dena Cushenberry, hatched a plan. As a former principal of a Blue Ribbon school, Cushenberry's creative response was to use a futures orientation, not a problem-solving approach.

She devised a plan to redistrict poverty and racial imbalances occurring naturally within the district's housing patterns and a way to scale up the district's eight-step instructional model that increased instructional time for struggling students. Then she led the charge to redistrict and balance the entire swath of eleven K–5 and three middle schools into a K–4 and 5–8 alignment of twelve schools. At the same time, the district leadership team implemented a year-round calendar of nine weeks on, two weeks off, giving students lagging behind an extra twenty days of instructional time and providing enrichment for those students who needed it.

In 2012, Cushenberry, now superintendent, won a coveted $28.6-million-dollar Race to the Top grant, one of sixteen in the nation, to extend Warren's eight-step instructional model deeply into personalized, technology-supported, one-to-one learning environments for all students.

This story illustrates the actions of educators in hot water—how a school leader translates a crisis into positive change. Malcolm Gladwell, author of *The Tipping Point*, observed that such actions lead to exceptional and radical change, contrary to all expectations.

We all know exceptional leaders like Dr. Cushenberry. Perhaps you are one of them. In this book we capture the narratives of school leaders who, against some great odds, have found a way to build positive narratives in their schools. We present ways of organizing institutions to discover their positive core through Appreciative Inquiry (AI) theory and practices. AI schools and districts re-create the dreams and possibilities for students, staff, and their communities continuously.

We call the six spheres we created for this purpose appreciative organizing in public education.

Appreciative organizing (AO), using a positive strengths-based change process, is by definition generative. It taps into people's desire to make a difference in the lives of children and youths. This is the primary passion for most educators; it's why they entered the profession. It is why many veteran teachers stay up many nights planning, grading essays, and e-mailing colleagues. AO is a vehicle for creating positive narratives that can lead to inspired reasons for schooling. AO starts with leaders who hold themselves and others accountable to a clear and coherent purpose that benefits students, teachers, and the community. Organizational members who are committed to one another's learning and connected to the whole find learning and work fulfilling and are more resilient over time.

Relational leaders use generative learning to inspire the implementation of core values and purposes. They encourage and build capacity by co-constructing new knowledge, skills, and practices that accelerate student learning. Relational leadership, positivity, and generativity are Appreciative Inquiry at its best.

We can fuel our imagination and inspire others by shining a light on where success is already happening. Marge Schiller writes *in Exceeding Expectations: An Anthology of Appreciative Inquiry Stories in Education from Around the World*:

> Education has been framed as a problem fraught with adversities. I think it's time to cut that out. This is the time to re-frame education as a great opportunity; a chance to understand what works well for children, families and communities. We need to extend and expand models of success.[1]

## OVERVIEW OF THE SIX SPHERES OF APPRECIATIVE ORGANIZING IN PUBLIC EDUCATION

The work presented here is based upon a growing core of literature and practitioner knowledge of AI, which is a form of positive organizational scholarship and practice. It comes out of a dialogue that took place around my coffee table in Tampa, Florida, as the authors attempted to design a new series of seminars and project-based learning interventions for a group of fifty-five assistant principals from six Florida counties. We took our inspiration from David Cooperrider's and others' work on AI theory and practice and from the writings of Michael Fullan and Carolyn Shields on educational leadership and created our six spheres for appreciative organizing in public education.

Linda, John, and I created the six spheres on chart paper taped to my mantel. It is our belief that AO is a vehicle for creating positive narratives that can lead to an inspired vision for schooling. The figure we designed in Tampa represents the dynamic interaction of six spheres, each representing an essential element of successful practice. The book is presented in chapters that correspond to our six spheres of the AO framework. In each chapter we define key terms and the roots of Appreciative Inquiry and positive organizational scholarship that our research and practice is based upon.

## APPRECIATIVE ORGANIZING IN PUBLIC EDUCATION:
A framework for learning, working, and living well together

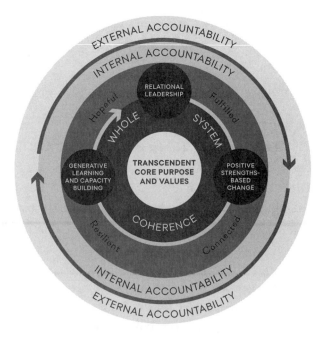

© 2014 Leonard C. Burrello, Linda M. Beitz, and John L. Mann

Figure 1: Transcendent Core Purposes and Values in an AO framework for Public Education

**First sphere: Transcendent Core Purposes and Values.**

Commentators Neil Postman,[2] Kenneth Strike,[3] Carol Shields,[4] and others have referred to transcendent core purposes and values that promote positive and fulfilling reasons for schooling in pursuit of the well being of all. Core purposes and values invite meaningful education outcomes when teams explore the positive core of their schools and districts. They connect their experiences in the school community to the core purpose and values. They clarify school and community visions of learning that optimally prepare students to fully engage in their own learning and the learning of others. Often the missing link in school district frameworks, core purposes and values drive and is driven by internal accountability. Jim Collins, the author of *Good to Great*, and his Stanford colleague Jerry Porras have called linking purpose and core values "the core ideology" of the organization. Yes, words create worlds!

**Second sphere: A Positive Strength-Based Change.**

A positive strength-based change process is the means by which a school community develops and sustains its stated purposes and core values. It is further used to guide the discovery, design, and implementation of practices that will prepare students. For example, a purpose statement might be "to prepare literate, civil-minded critical thinkers who are socially and ethically responsible to ensure the well being of all members of the school and community."

**Third sphere: Relational Leadership.**

Relational leadership requires leaders who can unleash the potential of all members of the school community to engage students, families, and community in their moral compact to educate students. A fulfilled and desired future grows out of coming to know one another's individual narratives while appreciating each other's individual gifts, differences, and perspectives.

Together these elements create the foundation for community life in and out of school. This charges leaders to ignite conversations and actions as trust builders. Leaders using generative learning processes build internal creative responses that make the purpose, values, and vision for schools come alive. This co-construct of the strategies and interventions to prepare all students regardless of class, gender, race, ethnicity, sexual orientation, or (dis)ability leads to deeper commitment and implementation with fidelity.

### Fourth sphere: Generative Learning and Capacity Building.

There are six mind-sets that Innovation Partners International offers to illustrate what relational leaders do as part of this sphere. Innovation Partners International[5] has translated these mind-sets in six deeply moving capacities: *Radical appreciation of others; Disruptive inquiry; Potent possibilities; Elegant design; Agile action; and Perpetual evolution.* These are the processes through which teams learn about their schools and reframe the future, being affirmative and visualizing positive possibilities. They work together collaboratively to determine what makes the school or district work (the positive core) and what can make it better. Building capacity allows schools to respond to emergent legislative, technological, and sociocultural changes that press for accountability for all students. School teams operate in an environment of constant change and complexity driven by outside forces that need to be balanced against a school's internal accountability values.

### Fifth sphere: Managing Internal and External Accountability.

Public education is characterized by a high level of fluid participation from multiple stakeholders who oftentimes make different claims on institutions. System leaders are required to continuously create disparate pathways to success for all learners. Schools are bombarded with high-stakes external accountability pressures from state and federal agencies. The key leadership function here is managing the paradoxical internal and external accountability expectations. A unifying purpose based on a core set of values guides staff with diverse perspectives. System leaders create the space for implementation of innovations that do not overwhelm its people and systems.

### Sixth sphere: Whole System Coherence.

Without deliberate and concentrated effort, whole system coherence falters. Whole system coherence is the energizing force that sustains high levels of success and engagement. Stakeholders (students, teachers, principals, and community members) know how their contributions are valued and are invited to learn how to participate in school and student learning. Stakeholder engagement is a measure of success. We believe hopefulness, connectedness, resiliency, and fulfillment are the four qualitative outcomes that lead to well being. These qualities provide the "glue" that holds the organization together. This entails keeping the whole system in front of the school and community rather than meeting the individual needs of one stakeholder. It means operationalizing the work of schools through adaptive leadership and technical management.

## THE PURPOSES OF THIS BOOK

AI theory has already contributed significantly to the positive change revolution in many professional realms, such as the armed services, United Nations, and Fortune 500 businesses. Now, we want to directly apply AI theory to public education through an appreciative organizing framework. We invite educators and their community members to join us in exploring the application of AO. The positive change movement has much to offer the evolution of public education. Creating positive narratives in public education can reconnected stakeholders to their community. These are narratives of growth, not decay; narratives of opportunity, not inequity; and narratives of excellence, not mediocrity. We believe this book can assist school leaders in establishing and promoting a transcendent moral purpose to unify all stakeholders with a common agenda to serve the well being of all students.

We want this book to be part of a larger conversation about the role of AO in public schools. We provide an antidote to the popular narratives put out by governors, state legislatures, and media who see public education as a failed institution. We call this change movement the Transformative Narratives Project. We've developed the website AOeducation.net to capture and share the stories of school leaders who are building alternative success narratives. We also offer professional development and certification. We will continue to share our discoveries and our ongoing work in schools, districts, and states. On behalf of Linda and John, I invite you to join the Transformative Narratives Project.

— Leonard C. Burrello
Tampa, Florida

# CHAPTER ONE
## The First Sphere of AO
### Creating Transcendent Core Purposes and Values
Leonard C. Burrello

*Fully engaged individuals forged in relationship to one another sharing*
*a common purpose gives meaning to their lives and those of others.*
—Daniel James Brown, *The Boys in the Boat*

Noted public commentator Neil Postman writes in *The End of Education*, "What makes the public schools public is not so much that the schools have common goals but that the students have common values. The reason for this is that public education does not serve the public. It creates a public . . . and what kind of a public does it create?"[1] He offers multiple possibilities: "A conglomerate of self-indulgent consumers? Angry, soulless, directionless masses? Indifferent, confused citizens? Or a public imbued with confidence, a sense of purpose, a respect for learning, and tolerance?"[2] The answer to these questions, Postman argues, "has nothing to do with the on-going reform discussions of class size, standardized testing, teacher accountability, school grades, school re-structuring or other methods of the management of schools."[3] He offers that the only answer, the right answer, lies in two things: "the existence of shared narratives and the capacity of such narratives to provide an inspired reasoning for schooling."[4]

Postman sets the stage for the next generation of questions. Particularly, can we educate all children to high levels in spite of deficit orientations? Can we include students of poverty, color, or disabilities? Can we maintain a public system of schools in spite of the corporate takeover of public education—a takeover by corporations that might have separate goals, and more importantly, create separate publics that do not know or care about each other? Postman observes that almost everybody is unhappy about the ways things are that is why we inquire into the future and we experiment. For Postman, the American experiment is a fine and noble but imperfect story. It can and does leave children out and often does not respect cultural differences. It is full of mistakes, and some successes—social security comes to mind. But can the American experiment, with our revisions, be the inspiring story that creates the reason for learning? Appreciative organizing is a vehicle for creating those positive narratives that can lead to inspired reasons for schooling.

Businesses leaders, elected officials, and media commentators blame the schools for being inadequate, declaring schools not up to the task of preparing the next generation for a globally competitive world. They have promoted deficit rhetoric and bemoaned the shortcomings of public education. This hyperbolic commentary pushes education practitioners to the political and pedagogical margins. Public education is a uniquely American political institution, not a recent political phenomenon. It is useful to chronicle the historical and contemporary tensions and purposes of public education, and examine the beliefs pertaining to the future of public education as well. It is my contention that the deficit orientation and failure narrative of public education is accentuated by the national and state partisan political culture of our governance today. While the nation has had a long history of private education, the last twenty years have seen the growth of an emerging economic sector. A highly incentivized privatization movement has fostered competition between the private and public sectors. In legislative sessions and school board meetings this competition is referred to as "choice." Schools, curriculum and instructional materials, supplementary programs, cyberschools, and assessment and remedial interventions are all being supported by public policy and public dollars. The private sector need not adhere to the same oversight, rules, and regulations that govern public schools. So we have a developing three-level system of private, publicly supported private charters, and public schools.

## SETTING THE STAGE: THE HISTORICAL CONTEXT

The communal drive for public education predates the nineteenth century. Its origins lie in the sociocultural, political, and spiritual beliefs of our nation's Founding Fathers. While their beliefs, rightly or wrongly, on the matter of public education were informed by the social and political milieu of their time, it is nonetheless important for us to ask the searing question today: What do we mean by "public education"? Amid other considerations, public education has come to be defined as education—or schooling. Let's start with a definition. Nancy Kober, working with the Center on Education Policy, stated that public education is "publicly financed, tuition-free, accountable to public authorities, and accessible to all students being educated in all types of schools, traditional to charter and magnet, vocational, (virtual schools) and alternative schools."[5]

The chronicle of public education makes it evident that the pursuit of publicly financed education in the United States has been difficult historically. Public education has been attacked, neglected, praised, abandoned, and, in the minds of some, in need of a private market to create a pathway for competition. Kober argues that while we are concerned with improving student achievement, public education does not exist merely to provide private economic benefits like high-salary positions for individuals in a global economy. Public benefits, she believes should be a primary focus of public education. I have long found the economic imperative as sole impetus for public schooling in America to be shortsighted and actually damaging. The transformative narrative must address both the public good and private good education offers to the individual and society.[7]

The mission of public education was articulated early in our nation's history. Summarizing Kober's 2007 report, I identify a set of purposes and the historical eras in which they were first introduced into the public discourse. You will recognize many of the forward-thinking individuals who championed public education. (They've earned the moniker *forefather* for a reason.) The first six were identified in the CEP report, and the last two are trends making themselves felt in the present era.

## 1. To Prepare People for Citizenship in a Democratic Society (1779–1787)

One of the first mission statements for public education came from Thomas Jefferson. The third American president wrote in a letter to James Madison: "Above all things I hope the education of the common people will be attended to, convinced that on their good sense we may rely with the most security for the preservation of a due degree of liberty."[6] Jefferson requested that the Virginia legislature in 1779 create free elementary schools for all "white boys and girls" regardless of family income, and to go on to educate only the brightest boys through their teens. The legislature rejected the bill because they did not want to support the education of the poorest among them.[7] It's interesting to note that one of the first conflicts over public education is rooted in social class and racial differences.

Thirty years earlier in 1749, Benjamin Franklin wrote Jefferson that a good education is

> . . . the sure foundation of the happiness of both private families and of commonwealths. Government should find it wise and the object of their responsibility to establish and endow with proper revenues seminaries of

learning . . . to serve the public with honor to themselves, and to their country.[8]

Here, Franklin calls for the creation of a public institution whose unification would lead to shared values taught in schools endowed with public funds. Fareed Zakaria writing in his book, *In Defense of Public Education*, noted that Jefferson's political opponent, the conservative John Adams was supportive of the public funding of education. Adams wrote, "The whole people must take upon themselves the education of the whole people, and must be willing to bear the expense of it." Adams further believed that "There should not be a district of mile square without a school in it, not founded by a charitable individual, but maintained at the public expense of the people themselves." Zakaria noted that Jefferson's fear was without a public system of education, the country would end up be ruled by a privileged elite that would maintain its advantages through a private network of institutions.[9]

### 2. To Improve Social Conditions (1786)

Writing in 1786, Benjamin Rush, a physician and statesperson, argued that the state would spend less on prisons when youth were properly educated. The money spent on incarceration was more than enough to maintain public schools. Rush's observation is foreboding when we examine present incarceration statistics of adults of color and school dropouts. According to Kober, "most prison inmates are high school dropouts, including 75% of state prison inmates, 59% of federal inmates, and 69% of jail inmates did not complete high school."[10] Her policy brief further argues

> that early advocates of the common school put great store in the power of public education to eliminate poverty, crime, and a host of other social problems. Although education has not done away with all of society's ills, it

has clearly improved people's lives according to a variety of social indicators. People with more education are less likely than undereducated adults to commit crimes, be homeless, or abuse drugs, to cite just a few examples. Those with more education enjoy better health and more stable families.[11]

Education can equalize opportunity and reduce adverse consequences for society.

## 3. To Unify a Diverse Population (1836)

In 1836, theologian and abolitionist Calvin Stowe wrote, "the most efficient, and indeed the only effectual way to produce this individuality and harmony of national feeling and character is to bring our children into the same schools and have them educated together."[12] Kober writes, "for two centuries, public schools have been the main institution in American society responsible for transmitting a common American culture to a diverse population. Public schools have been the place where immigrants have learned the English language and absorbed American culture and values. Views have shifted over time about how best to promote unity while respecting diverse cultures."[13] In *The End of Education: Redefining the Value of School*, Neil Postman calls this purpose the "American Experiment."

Historically, U.S. public schools like its counterparts in New Zealand and Canada are challenged to fulfill the mission of unifying more diverse populations of students. Part of building a common culture involves teaching students from different racial, ethnic, religious, and economic backgrounds to respect each other. Early advocates of the common school movement, believed that when children from different backgrounds shared in a common education, class conflict would disappear and people would interact with greater civility. Public schools continue to be the chief institution that brings together young people from diverse backgrounds, much like the armed forces did through the Vietnam draft. Although many private and public charter schools enroll a diverse student body, they are typically less diverse than public schools. Private and charter schools do not have the same responsibility to forge a cohesive society. They simply have not historically educated all children together.

Today, the mission of promoting cultural unity while respecting differences in class, race, gender, sexual orientation, ethnicity, and ability is more crucial than ever. The population of the United States has become more ethnically and linguistically diverse at the same time that the economy has become more global and technically demanding. In fact, in 2015, the minority population in the nation's public schools is approaching the white majority. And in a world simultaneously beset with ethnic strife and growing smaller, the ability to understand other perspectives and deal with conflict are critical skills for students to master.

## 4. To Prepare People to Become Economically Independent (1848)

The man known as the father of the common school, Horace Mann, wrote in 1848, "education, then, beyond all other devices of human origin, is the great equalizer of the conditions of men—the balance-wheel of the social machinery. It does better than disarm the poor of their hostility towards the rich; it prevents being poor."[14] Here, equity, opportunity, and the prevention of poverty for all are the chief rationales for the common public school. Economic arguments have historically provided persuasive reasons for maintaining and improving American public education, and such arguments draw strong public support. As people know from their own experience and research reports, individual earnings are strongly linked to educational attainment beyond high school. But is that sufficient as our sole purpose?

In particular, public high schools, unlike the vast majority of private schools, offer vocational and technical education for students who learn best through hands-on, problem-based instruction not necessarily leading to a four-year college degree. Being inclusive of all students regardless of dis/ability and preparedness for post-school life meets community and commercial needs of the American economy. As mentioned, this is a primary reason for the establishment of a public system to serve all students—"to justify the creation of public schools, early advocates often emphasized the economic benefits of education."[15] Providing the children of the poor and middle class with an education would prepare them to obtain good jobs, which in turn would reduce disparities in wealth and strengthen the nation's economic growth. Without a question, public education has been the engine of upward economic mobility for millions of Americans.

Since most Americans attend public schools, the quality of the public education system not only affects an individual's ability to get a good job but also shapes the nation's ability to compete in a global economy. As many developing nations understand quite well, investing in public education is one of the surest means to improving a nation's economic standing. While the United States has historically had a higher number of college graduates, it has slipped from number one in world rankings to the middle or high teens.

## 5. To Provide Universal Access to Free Education (1883)

Frederick Douglass, writing in 1883, suggested that "the whole country is directly interested in the education of every child that lives within its borders. The ignorance of any part of American people so deeply concerns all the rest that there can be no doubt of the right to pass laws compelling the attendance of every child at school."[16]

Free universal access to education remains as necessary a condition today as it was 125 years ago for Americans to lead morally, socially, and economically viable lives. Public schools educate the vast majority of American students and will continue to do so for the foreseeable future. Public schools are accessible in all parts of the country, including areas where few private or public charter schools exist. Private schools, including the new charter movement, though important to many families, were not designed to be a universal system. Two notable exceptions are New Orleans and Detroit. Both are struggling with few success stories.

### 6. To Guarantee Equal Opportunities for All Children (1900)

Civil rights leader Susan B. Anthony wrote, "a republican government should be based upon free and equal education among the people."[17] Kober argues in her policy brief that "public education has long been recognized as a gateway to opportunity for people from all economic and racial/ethnic backgrounds. Early advocates of public education contended that only public funding would give schools the consistent support needed to educate children from poor families and bring a more standard approach to curriculum, length of the school year, teacher qualifications, and other characteristics. In later years, advocates for the rights of women and minorities saw public schools as the institution with the greatest capacity to improve people's futures and change public attitudes."[18]

Reducing the disparities in educational achievement and graduation rates in many urban and some rural communities goes beyond the capacity of the school alone to meet the needs of children and families. Many scholars have written about the need to engage other social/public services to provide an additional twelve hours of support on top of the six-hour school day.

Although public schools have become more inclusive, equal access to high-quality education is not yet a reality. Wide differences exist among schools, districts, and states in per-pupil funding, the availability of experienced or highly qualified teachers, the effectiveness of leadership, and the access to advanced courses and technology. Michael Flanagan, the former state superintendent of Michigan, argues that education alone can solve the larger problems of society. He believes "we must confront a harsh truth that when our children are facing insurmountable problems outside of school, it will be virtually impossible for us to educate them inside of school and as a society, we have to care enough to make sure all students are able to come to school and learn."[19]

## 7. Education for All Handicapped Children Act (1975)

In 1975 a tremendous coalition of parents, educators, and politicians at state and national levels came together for the first time in our history to guarantee public education for students with disabilities. President Ford's signature ensured that every child with a disability would have space provided for them in the public schools regardless of the type and severity of disability. For the past forty years, the federal government has promised a 40 percent level of funding for these students. The number never reached more than 18 percent. Federal funds total about 9 to 11 percent of all funds spent on public education. Full membership of these students in typical public school classes has been and remains a highly controversial issue since regulations were promulgated in 1977.[20]

## 8. College and Career Readiness and the Common Core (2010)

The most recent and almost universally accepted purpose for public education was stated in speeches to the National Governors Association in 2004. Former Microsoft chairman and now philanthropist Bill Gates argued for national standards to enhance America's standing in the world community. Forty-eight governors originally opted to sign on for the establishment and assessment of common core standards. Governors from approximately forty states have maintained a commitment to their implementation. The same historical forces that have shaped public policy in the United States for 225 years have shaken the coalition of governors endorsing the Common Core. State level critics argue that federal intrusion into state educational policy has exceeded its constitutional mandate. Of course, that argument seems disingenuous, given it was the governors who initiated the Common Core. The department of education and Race to the Top grab the headlines, but Common Core policy is directed at the state level.[21]

Harvard political scientist and philosopher Michael Sandel provides a fitting summary to the mission of public education. "A democracy does not require perfect equality but it does require that citizens share in a common life. What matters is that people of different backgrounds and social positions encounter one another, and bump up against one another, in the course of everyday life. Because this is how we learn to negotiate and abide our differences, and how we come to care for the common good."[22]

What makes public education so crucial today is its "publicness," in contrast to the neoconservative or neoliberal embrace of market principles. Education's central challenge is to serve an ever-expanding public—living well with people from diverse cultures and perspectives. The privatization advocates share no such commitment. They can exclude anyone they choose. Public schools continue to be the preeminent place for individuals to learn how to live well together now and in the future. The public school may be the last public institution that encourages the coming together of diverse populations to understand different perspectives and value systems.

## GETTING TO CORE PURPOSES AND VALUES

There is no one purpose or set of values to which all school communities must subscribe. Relational leader John Mann advises new leaders to use the Why, How, and What as a means of framing core purposes and values early on in their tenure.

### Getting to the Why of AO

Getting to core purposes and values starts with a belief that we human beings have the capacity to create the futures we want for ourselves and others. What is our preferred future? Why do we pursue what we pursue? Simon Sinek, the author of *Start with Why: How Great Leaders Inspire Everyone to Take Action*, teaches that "people don't buy what you do but why you do it." The nobleness of the mission, established by multiple stakeholders, brings people on board. The work of the school or district is guided by core purposes created together. The purpose and values that undergird its pursuit make up the district or school's core ideology. Working in schools, I taught the concept of a "good enough vision." It didn't have to be perfect, but it did require hard decisions about values central to making the vision a reality in the everyday life of the schools.

### Getting to the How of AO

The how of AO is about inquiring into organizational life through active exploration and discovery. It means asking questions; being open to new potentials leading to real possibilities. The how continues through designing responses and implementing. Teams learn during implementation to revisit, revise, and to try again.

### Getting to the What of AO

The what of AO is about valuing—and recognizing—the best in people and the world around you. It requires relational leaders who affirm past and present strengths and successes. The people who will eventually implement prototypes or interventions actually build them. Leaders take care that their community members are given what they need to bring life, health, vitality, and commitment to excellence. Finally, it's about an increase in the value of an education, e.g., the economy has appreciated in value so now your education means more, versus your education means more because of your investment in it.

### Getting There Is Half the Fun

In an AO organization all stakeholders are invited to join in the work of the school in a quest to discover their core purposes and values. The core values are a set of principles to guide decision-making in pursuit of the schools' purpose. They guide actions of leadership—including saying no when a a grant offer is in conflict with the core purposes and values of the district. Case Western professor David Cooperrider writes, "organizations move in the direction of their most compelling guiding images of the future."[23] The key to making the vision come alive is gaining the commitment and engagement of stakeholders. It is not *what* the vision says that matters; it's what the vision *does* to motivate people to act in concert. For example, often all members cannot, or do not, participate in establishing the vision for the school or district.

Dr. Lynn Murray, a principal of a K–8 school in Williston, Vermont, joined the district after an innovative team of teachers and the school board created the school's vision featuring a personalized learning strategy and parental choice. Her task was to get the rest of the faculty onboard—those who were not engaged in vision development. She wisely came up with an analogy for the staff to consider. She advised the remaining nine teacher teams to see the original vision as a destination they were traveling toward. She encouraged each team to learn from the trailblazers, the SWIFT team, however, their task was to create their own pathway to reach that destination. She explained,

> . . . it's like we are all traveling to Denver, but each team must determine how you want to get there, and what do you and your students want to experience along the way. How many different pathways can we generate? What new possibilities have you considered? Why this path?[24]

Dr. Murray tied together the work of the ten teams through a fourteen-person school leadership team that included staff members from each grade level.

First, her focus was on collaboration within and between teams with a clear message. The Williston teams' study and deliberation was an affirming inquiry into how to design engaging project-based learning strategies into their curriculum. They co-constructed their designs with parents and students. Their goal was to produce "a self-reinforcing, synergistic relationship between creating strategy, learning through the process, and producing the results."[25]

We tracked the Williston story over twelve years. It provides insights into the AI/AO process, starting with "asking unconditional positive questions . . . generating new learning about the resources that make their organizing and action possible."[26] Murray and her leadership team strengthened the relational bonds within and between the ten teams. Together they translated vision into reality, and through the process they "created new levels of commitment to action. Consequently, as process and results are maximized in the same moment, results are achieved much more quickly."[27] Within two years, Murray had nine teams functioning in alignment with the vision. The tenth team chose to go a more traditional way, gradually lost enrollment, and was dissolved. Williston maintained a sustainable process at the school for many years. They learned to accommodate No Child Left Behind and Common Core requirements for more linear programming, especially in mathematics. Murray and her school-wide leadership team "remained cognizant of its conversational streams and sought to influence them at the levels of relational leadership."[28] She worked through team leaders to maintain a coherent system of team support and development—like increasing student and parent satisfaction with a range of teaching teams to choose from. The school was always above the state average, and their ongoing use of data drove midstream program corrections to maintain high levels of achievement and well-being.

## LIVING WELL TOGETHER

Over the last thirty years, I have learned that school strategic planning teams can pinpoint purpose, values, and vision regardless of the range of stakeholders from inside and outside the school district. The real question is why do they want to change and what do they want to change? What futures do the stakeholders seek and value the most? In my work I ask mixed groups of professionals, parents, and community stakeholders to generate three separate lists: purpose, values, and vision statements. The groups discover that the lists overlap, and they quickly reach consensus on their meaning and worth. Ownership grows when individuals in each group see how their own personal beliefs have emerged through a democratic process. Once the process is established, priority setting across all sets of statements moves quickly and creates a deeper level of commitment to the end result.

Bringing outside world perspectives into the deliberations is key to creating rich, generative conversations. These perspectives should take into consideration the current reality of the school, the district, the community, and the state context. Often there are conflicts between internal and external priorities—conflicts that must be addressed to reach a consensus on the future. And too often schools and districts rely on external consultants and incentives to drive their planning process. The AO process engages the hearts and minds of all stakeholders to drive thinking about the future. Environment scanning has an important place in the preparation of purpose and core values by offering alternative perspectives. To be most effective, finding the positive core of the district or school should be the first objective. For example, it took about one day for a group of fifty-two district leaders in Meridian, Mississippi, to rediscover core values in their district. A historical work ethic surfaced as a core value. Centering work ethic into a purpose statement was an essential unifying value that all fifty-two district leaders could agree on. It was a building block that would engender teacher and community resonance later.

I agree with Michael Mantel and James Ludema that leaders ensure sustainability by shaping the organizational "conversational streams and extending appreciative inquiry from a one-time or periodic intervention technique into a continuous philosophical approach facilitated by leadership development and organization design."[29] Initiating new conversations that build upon historical conversations enable leaders to reveal the organizations' positive core. Each unique school or district possesses a matrix of strengths that provide the foundation for a new beginning. Generative learning processes sustain AI groups—ongoing learning and revising increases the probability of reaching their collective future. School people have been historically optimistic about their ability to make a difference in the lives of children. But over the last twenty-seven years educators have been in the "permanent white water" of educational reform—the rapids of new mandates and social challenges rushing around every bend in the river.

In Meridian, we worked to discover the positive core of the district and its schools as an essential starting point. The superintendent committed to new leadership development and organization design of district and school-based interventions. Here's how we did it. In order to establish trust and ensure freedom of expression and commitment, the district leadership team was engaged in planning backward from the future into the present. Each group member was assigned to a goal-based work group based upon their expertise, interests, or jurisdiction. Each of the five teams met monthly, led by a district- and school-based co-facilitator, to create their intervention and implementation plan. The plans were evaluated based on their clarity, feasibility, and relevance and built into a fidelity plan for each intervention. Working together, the groups reached a collective commitment to make the Meridian Compass, their framework name, a reality.[30]

The stability of leadership and staff is crucial to school and district success. I have learned that team stability is maintained through a belief in district and school purposes. Such belief builds staff resiliency, enabling them to persist in light of external demands for accountability. The relational leaders' dedication to purpose fosters the trust and respect that leads to whole system coherence. "Living well and living well together," as Kenneth Strike suggests, is our common outcome for all system members and/or organizational stakeholders. District and school leadership need to take responsibility for instilling the four attributes of successful membership in an appreciative organization: hopefulness, connectedness, resiliency, and fulfillment. "Live together well." That's a motto for an AO organization.[31]

The community summit exercise, similar to what was done in Meridian, is offered at the end of the book. It is a means of getting to an AI theory of action using a set of principles to guide district-school-community team development. Linda Beitz and I detail a district-level planning process and a community summit plan for whole-system engagement. Such processes engage top district- and school-level leadership and governance units, like the board of education or city/county councils, along with community representatives with a stake in the district's future.

A second exercise, the Root Causes of Success (rather than

the root causes of failure), builds upon our interpretation of Diane Whitney and others. John Mann and I developed an exercise to help individual leaders chronicle how, why, and in what ways they became successful. We provide a profile of an Indiana educator's journey from assistant principal to superintendent. This exercise takes about four hours to complete with an audience of fifty people working in teams of two and six.

Let's end the first sphere of AO back on the boat. In *The Boys in the Boat* Daniel James Brown introduces readers to George Pocock, a racing shell boat builder and rowing guru who helped the 1936 Olympic rowing crew from the University of Washington win an Olympic medal. Pocock recognized what a common goal does for a group of individuals who bond to a purpose that goes beyond and above individual performance. This excerpt represents the ideal I am striving for. It represents an inclusive, interdependent, and collaborative community coming together for a singular purpose. It honors each team member's energy and their commitment to something greater than themselves. Each member derives satisfaction from the collaborative enterprise.

> [Pocock] learned much about the hearts and soul of young men. He learned to see hope where a boy thought there was no hope, to see skills where skill was obscured by ego or by anxiety. He observed the fragility of confidence and the redemptive power of trust. He detected the strength of the gossamer threads of affection that sometimes grew between a pair of young men among a boatload of them striving honestly to do their best. And he came to understand how those almost mystical bonds of trust and affection, if nurtured correctly, might lift a crew above the ordinary sphere, transport it to a place where nine boys somehow became one thing—a thing that

could not quite be defined, a thing that was so in tune with the water and the earth and the sky above that, as they rowed, effort was replaced by ecstasy. It was a rare thing, a sacred thing, a thing devoutly to be hoped for.

# CHAPTER TWO
## The Second Sphere of AO
### Positive Strengths-Based Change: A Revolution in Organizing
By Linda M. Beitz

*Every few hundred years in Western history there occurs a sharp transformation. Within a few short decades, society — its world view, its basic values, its social and political structure, its arts, its key institutions — rearranges itself . . . We are currently living through such a time.*
—Peter Drucker

## SETTING THE STAGE

From 1946 up until 1991, my family owned the oldest bowling alley in the city of Chicago, Southport Lanes. It was housed in a Schlitz building—because back then breweries built their own shops—with manual pinsetters in a working-class neighborhood. My grandparents lived upstairs and Grandma tended bar into her eighties. She came downstairs when Dad went up for supper and a nap so he would be able to keep working into the wee hours of the morning. Everyone called her Ma. My mom and dad ran the place and made their living by ensuring Leo and Ella's Southport Lanes had camaraderie and fun. It was the spot neighborhood people wanted to be. And my parents were successful. Not money rich, but community rich. I spent a lot of time at the bowling alley up until my twenties. I watched my parents navigate the personalities of the folks who walked in the door. Mom knitted people together. She offered big buffets so people would wander over after ball games in neighboring Wrigley Field. She also had an uncanny ability to connect with people. She asked questions, listened attentively, and they shared their life story. Dad presumed positive intent from everyone, and his generosity of spirit, good humor, and playfulness was what Chicagoans needed. He could teach anyone to bowl.

The bedrock my brothers and I learned from watching our parents work was that relationships and integrity matter. Success is founded on it. It will make or break how you feel and think about your work—and your life. Perhaps as a result of my early experiences, I've been intensely curious about what makes a successful organization tick—and for me that translated to educational organizations. What keeps people connected to one another? What drives their desire to be the best that they can be in their organizational lives, individually or collectively? I take to heart statistics about the majority of people in the world being disengaged at work. I've crafted a life of ongoing learning aimed at cultivating a way of thinking, being, and doing that could transform this state of affairs. My introduction to Appreciative Inquiry provided me with "just in time learning."

In 2011 I had recently transitioned from administrative work in education and was in the newest chapter of my career as a mediator and consultant, facilitating dialogues between groups and individuals experiencing conflict. I received a newsletter from Champlain College, and President David Finney's column grabbed my attention. He described how in August the college had invited over four hundred people from throughout Vermont—students, parents, trustees, employers, government officials, career counselors, faculty, and staff—to participate in a summit titled "Building Partnerships for a Thriving Workforce!" The honorary chair of the summit was Bob Stiller, well known in Vermont and across the globe as the founder and then board chair of Vermont-based Green Mountain Coffee Roasters (GMCR), now Keurig Green Mountain. The summit was framed around the principles and practices of AI. Stiller had employed AI principles and practices at GMCR, to which he directly attributed the company's success.

Given the preponderance of problem-solving models in the research and practice of organizational development (including my own work at the time), I was intrigued by the definition of AI: "Appreciative Inquiry deliberately links strength-based thinking with the full spectrum of stakeholders, encouraging positive sharing of ideas, mutual learning, and listening to one another." It conjured up a compelling image of moving an entire system forward in an optimistic, energetic, creative, and powerful way.

Within two weeks of reading that newsletter, I enrolled in the AI Practitioner Program at the Weatherhead School of Management at Case Western Reserve University. The course was inspirational. It provided me with new theories, principles, and practices to innovate my work. AI theory's focus on positive strengths-based change resonated with me—purposefully shifting away from endeavoring to "fix" an organization's deficiencies and toward identifying the system's strengths, identifying the "points of pride," then building upon and expanding those strengths in service of the affirmative direction stakeholders imagine.

From that place of inspiration, I returned to work in 2012 in public education when Leonard Burrello introduced me to colleagues at the University of Kansas who had recently received the Schoolwide Integrated Framework for Transformation (SWIFT) Center grant. The grant is a 24.5-million-dollar federal investment intended to transform how public education is engineered and delivered to meet the needs of each and every child. My first big (read *really* big) opportunity to carry forward some of my new AI learning was when I was hired to join that team to co-coordinate the design and implementation of the grant's inaugural professional learning institute, which we titled "Building the Foundation: Partnering for Excellence and Equity in Education." Using the SOAR (Strengths, Opportunities, Aspirations, and Results) strategic planning model, an outgrowth of AI theory and practice (detailed later in this chapter) developed by Jacqueline Stavros and Gina Hinrichs, our launch team crafted a multiday event for over two hundred individuals from across our system. That system included teams representing each of our partner states (Maryland, New Hampshire, Mississippi, Oregon and Vermont), our federal partners (US Department of Education / Office of Special Education Programs), our knowledge development sites, and a myriad of other stakeholders with a vested interest in the success of our work. It stands as one of the most gratifying professional development experiences of my career, due in part to our keeping fidelity to a strengths-based approach in our event design and getting a sizable segment of the system in the room to collectively engage in creating a future for our partnership. Our state and local partners were relieved that we were going to focus on strengths and opportunities and not engage in a process of identifying what was broken or deficient about their educational organizations. At the close of this national launch, the positive energy and inspiration in the room for the grant partners' future work together was palpable. Building on the successes of the work being done by the SWIFT Center and the incorporation of AI into the training of assistant principals in several Florida counties, we conceptualized our framework and this book.

## ABOUT THIS CHAPTER

The intent of the sections that follow is to create shared understanding of the underpinnings of our framework for appreciative organizing in public education and to deepen our inquiry about its potential in expanding and sustaining positive change in our public school systems. First, I aim to provide a review and reflection on some select organizational change literature focused on the question: "What is the world asking of organizations now that is different from how we have designed organizational models and ways of organizing in the past?" Second, to identify from this research and analysis the shared "shifts" in thinking, being, and doing in organizational life that collectively comprise a revolution in organizing, a revolution aligned with a positive, generative, and strengths-based theory of change. Finally, to suggest some questions for imagining new possibilities for public education in America based on the successes of positive organizational scholarship in practice—most notably AI.

My greatest hope is that you will discover for yourself actionable pathways that will contribute to making our public schools and educational systems places where our students, families, staff, and stakeholders can fulfill their aspirations and build a better world in the process.

## PERSPECTIVES ON ORGANIZATIONAL MODELS AND WAYS OF ORGANIZING FOR CHANGE

Since the 1980s, new perspectives on ways of organizing and organizational models have emerged, representing nothing short of a revolution in thinking, being, and doing relative to how we design our organizational structures and organizational practices to effect change. All arrows point to a future view that has at its core life-centric purposes and positive, strengths-based theory and practices.

### The Evolution of Organizational Models

Can we create organizations free of the pathologies that show up all too often in the workplace? Free of the politics, bureaucracy, and infighting; free of the posturing at the top and drudgery at the bottom? Is it possible to reinvent organizations, to devise a new model that makes work productive, fulfilling, and meaningful? Can we create soulful workplaces—schools, hospitals, businesses, and non-profits—where our talents can blossom and our callings be honored?
—Frederic Laloux[1]

In his book *Reinventing Organizations*, Frederic Laloux provides an analysis of organizational models past and present that mirror the development of our consciousness as human beings and give us a window into future possibilities for organizations and organizing. In Table 2.1 below, Laloux summarizes four organizational models, their breakthroughs, and the dominant metaphors that contribute to his thinking about an emerging fifth organizational model and metaphor—a model he suggests is more fully in tune with what humanity needs now in our current stage of consciousness. He refers to these as TEAL organizations.[2] I offer Laloux's work here not as truth but as a perspective for reflection and inquiry that crosses multiple boundaries in ways of knowing, e.g., human evolution, developmental psychology, history, philosophy, science, and more.

Table 2.1 LALOUX FOUR ORGANIZATIONAL MODELS

| STAGE | CURRENT EXAMPLES | KEY BREAK-THROUGHS | GUIDING METAPHOR |
|---|---|---|---|
| **RED organizations** Constant exercise of power by the chief to keep troops in line. Fear is the glue of the organization. Highly reactive, short-term focus. Thrives in chaotic environments. | • Mafia • Street gangs • Tribal militias | • Division of labor • Command authority | • Wolf pack |
| **AMBER organizations** Highly formal roles within a hierarchal pyramid. Top-down command and control (what and how). Stability valued above all through rigorous processes. Future is a repetition of the past. | • Catholic Church • Military • Most government agencies • Public school systems | • Formal roles *(stable and scalable hierarchies)* • Processes *(long term perspectives)* | • Army |
| **ORANGE organizations** Goal is to beat the competition; achieve profit and growth. Innovation is the key to staying ahead. Management by objectives (command and control on what; freedom on the how) | • Multinational companies • Charter schools | • Innovation • Accountability • Meritocracy | • Machine |

| | | | |
|---|---|---|---|
| **GREEN organizations**<br>Within the classic pyramid structure, focus on culture and empowerment to achieve extraordinary employee motivation | Culture driven organizations (e.g., Southwest Airlines, Ben and Jerry's, etc.) | Empowerment<br>• Values-driven culture<br>• Stakeholder model | Family |
| **TEAL organizations** | ? | ? | ? |

Much of *Reinventing Organizations* focuses on filling in the question marks in Laloux's chart above based on his study of what he purports to be pioneer Teal organizations—spanning the globe and ranging in size from four hundred to forty thousand employees. Consider the major breakthroughs he identifies from his case studies as characterizing those organizations:

- Self-management—a system based on peer relationships without the need for either hierarchy or consensus

- Wholeness—bringing all of whom we are to work vs. distinguishing between our professional and personal being; welcoming the emotional, intuitive, and spiritual parts of ourselves; sharing our vulnerability as a strength, not a weakness

- Evolutionary purpose—rather than trying to predict and control the future, members of the organization are included in the process of listening for and co-creating the purpose the organization wants to serve[3]

Embedded in these breakthroughs are several significant shifts for the individual:

- From fear fueling the ego—to trust in the abundance of life

- From external factors largely governing our decision making—to inner rightness as our compass

- From pursuit of love, recognition and success based on what others think—to knowing our self and becoming the truest expression of that self

- From anger, shame or blame when roadblocks are met—to obstacles as lessons to be learned and appreciated for what they can teach us

- From noticing and focusing on what's wrong and/or broken—to a strengths based paradigm focusing on the good that is present and its potential for growth

- From facts and figures or rationality—to tapping wisdom evidenced in intuition, emotions and embracing the "both-and" thinking that lives in paradoxes[4]

The guiding metaphor Laloux offers for Teal organizations is a living organism or living system. "The metaphor opens up new horizons. Imagine what organizations would be like if we stopped designing them like soulless, clunky machines. What could organizations achieve, and what would work feel like, if we treated them like living beings, if we let them be fueled by the evolutionary power of life itself?"[5] Laloux takes inspiration for his metaphor from Margaret Wheatley, well-known author and management consultant, and her coauthor, Myron Kellner-Rogers:

> Partnering with life, working with its cohering motions, requires that we take life's direction seriously. Life moves toward wholeness. This direction cannot be ignored or taken lightly. People do not respond for long to small and self-centered purposes or to self-aggrandizing work.

Too many organizations ask us to engage in hollow work, to be enthusiastic about small-minded visions, to commit ourselves to selfish purposes, to engage our energy in competitive drives . . . When we respond with disgust, when we withdraw our energy from such endeavors, it is a sign of our commitment to life and to each other.[6]

In considering each of the organizational models, it is important to avoid judgment (i.e., one is good and another bad) in terms of where your own organizational system and culture might fit. While the articulation of multiple stages reflects the development of our consciousness, each stage is contextually bound, and the organizational models that emerge function as an adaptive response to that context. Also, we might find ourselves moving vertically between stages based on our adaptation and developing horizontally within a stage as well. For example, an individual espousing a far right perspective, and another a far left perspective, might operate from the same conformist Amber world of certainties, yet come to opposite conclusions on almost every issue.[7]

Albeit theoretically complex, there is a lesson embedded in this work that seems to me dramatically simple: the more conscious we are, the more choices we have open to us to act in service of our vision of what's possible via the way we structure our organizations and how we relate as human beings in the process of organizing. For example, if our vision for our educational organizations is for them to be places where everyone thrives— students, staff, families, school communities alike—and we know that essential to achieving that vision is for all stakeholders to be engaged in decisions that affect them, then how can we structure our organizing for change to enable that to happen? Similarly, if we are conscious of the multiplicity of strengths that a diverse human ecosystem such as a school community can represent, then how can we organize ourselves to tap that rich capacity to contribute to its growth and development? Aligning our actions with our consciousness of what's possible (our vision) is critical.

Expanding on this further, my own anecdotal experience in talking to educators has been that there is a great yearning to turn the tide in America from a dominant focus on the external accountability demands that have come to dictate much of the structuring of our schools, to consciously nurturing ways of organizing that allow for a natural striving toward excellence to emerge. Excellence that emanates when human beings collectively commit to a set of core purposes and values for their work together in service to something bigger than themselves. While external accountability is not likely to go away anytime soon (and shouldn't), internal accountability will always trump external accountability when it comes to achieving results. Evidence of this abounds in schools where educational stakeholders actively attend to creating the shared commitments and trusting relationships foundational for success. In those contexts, people willingly hold themselves and each other accountable for achieving results without fear of negative reprisal. Morale is high and there is hopeful action being taken to continually innovate to meet academic and social needs.

From Laloux's research, I see internal accountability evidenced in the breakthrough of "self-management" he identifies in Teal organizations. I've selected a practice illustrative of self-management to inform how it plays out in those organizations: the "advice process."

> It is very simple: in principle, any person in the organization can make any decision. But before doing so, that person must seek advice from all the affected parties and people with expertise on the matter. The person is under no obligation to achieve a watered-down

compromise that accommodates everyone's wishes. But advice must be sought and taken into consideration. The bigger the decision, the wider the net must be cast, including, when necessary, the CEO or the board of directors. Usually, the decision maker is the person who noticed the issue or the opportunity or the person most affected by it.[8]

Benefits of the advice process include the creation of community, humility, learning, better decisions, and fun. Teal organizations cling to these values and themes. They are echoed in subsequent sections of this chapter through the voices of other practitioners and researchers.[9] Given the hierarchical structure of American schools, self-management might be a stretch for some educators to imagine, although maybe less so for Generation Y, many of who have come to expect it, only to be confronted by outdated, outworn structures and processes found in many educational organizations.

Going further down this self-management path, in *Yes to the Mess*, Frank Barrett, professor of management and global public policy at the Naval Postgraduate School (and an accomplished jazz musician who has traveled extensively with the Tommy Dorsey Orchestra), also speaks to self-management's value in achieving positive growth:

> It's often assumed that without singular direction, groups turn chaotic or unruly. What we are learning, though, is that without being guided by an outside entity or prescripted plan, a system can self-organize and produce even more efficient and effective outcomes. Think how different this model is from the one we have been taught. We were told that social systems need hierarchy to function and coordinate. But when birds flock, when

cities form and expand, there is no controlling singular force. Individuals act unpredictably, yet a coherent and productive organization emerges. Just as in jazz. The message is provocative: an emergent system is smarter than the individual members. And systems grow smarter over time. The jazz mind-set is one that recognizes the emerging coherence amid constant flux.[10]

In education, we might recognize Barrett's jazz metaphor and Laloux's self-management in the concept of distributed leadership. I'm reminded of a group of teachers I interviewed while I was visiting a school in the Midwest to learn more about its well-known positive culture. Here is a paraphrase of their message: "We don't have all of the formal communication structures that are suggested on some rubrics, we're communicating all the time and making changes based on what we think will get us the best results (for students and families). We don't have time for a lot of formal meetings, and they couldn't happen quickly enough for the fast-paced decision making we need. Our principal supports us because he trusts us to do what's best."

From Laloux's research we get a glimpse into the future that emerging Teal organizations can offer us. We can also reflect on how our evolution in consciousness might unfold to reshape multiple aspects of our society, including how we choose to design our public schools.

## SOCIETAL TRANSFORMATION—
## AN EMPOWERMENT FRAMEWORK

David Gershon's *Social Change 2.0: A Blueprint for Reinventing Our World* offers another perspective to widen our lens on organizing for change. Gershon organized the First Earth Run in 1986. He orchestrated forty-five heads of state and sixty-two countries to participate in keeping alive a flame that was carried around the world to represent a vision of living together in harmony—people and planet. Gershon uses that experience and three additional success stories of dramatic, large-scale social change to underpin his Empowerment Model and Methodology (shown below).[11] His model shares themes found in Laloux's research, Fritz's structural change model,[12] and Cooperrider, et al, to come.

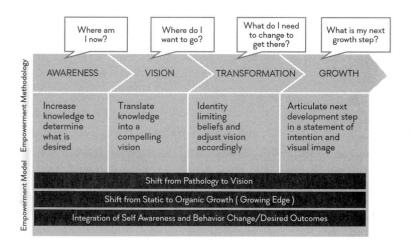

Foundational to Gershon's framework is the shift from pathology to vision, a shift to be made by both individuals and organizations. It seems safe to say that as human beings, we are far less motivated by what we don't want than by what we envision as a desirable future state. Positive images of the future can inspire us, give us hope, heal us, and catapult us forward into action. Conversely, if we see ourselves as broken and in need of fixing, the negative effects can work against our moving forward. This also applies to organizations. Gershon asserts, and I agree, that focusing on a positive vision is aligned with true transformation—creating new thinking, being, and doing in concert with the future we want to move into. With a lens focused only on the past, we can be limited and stuck trying to fix old problems with old approaches and solutions.[13]

Shifting from static to organic growth can best be summed up as the kind of growth that fuels our individual aliveness and the aliveness of our organizations as human enterprises. Individually or collectively, when we are growing in the direction of our dreams, we are more fulfilled. We can contribute to designing our "growth edge," as Gershon calls it, as we consider our vision and all the possibilities that it opens up for us, and then think through how we might act on the opportunities those possibilities suggest.[14] This "design" thinking involves considering what's desirable, viable, and feasible—developing and taking actions based on those criteria and then mindfully studying the results of those actions in implementation and revisiting the innovation process. Linking back to Barrett's jazz metaphor, essential to organic growth is having an improvisational mind-set, being "in action" and "in inquiry" simultaneously, constantly experimenting and assessing the results of our actions in relationship to our vision for change.

The integration of self-awareness and behavior change is the final foundational building block to Gershon's framework. It's comprised of the process that each individual must be willing to move through if change is to occur: awareness (assessment of current state); vision (an image of a desired future); transformation (thinking in the present in ways that represent that future); and growth (taking actions aligned with that thinking).[15]

Bottom line: it's one thing to become self-aware and another to productively act on that self-awareness.

Gershon asserts that limiting beliefs often block this essential integration and that surfacing those limiting beliefs is critical to accomplishing desired behavior change.[16] Bringing those beliefs (e.g., I'm not enough, it's hopeless, etc.) out into the open can be in and of itself a liberating act and create a new opening for change. It is often at this point that the support of others in seeing what we cannot see in ourselves is most valuable. Sharing our vulnerability as a strength, not weakness, opens up the path for others to do the same.

Gershon reconciled himself to the fact some time ago that we don't know what's not possible, so he's comfortable in the skin of someone who carries on making dreams happen. There are many elements of Gershon's framework that will look familiar to someone calling him or herself a change agent, beginning with the building of a collective vision of what might be, not based on what is, but rather fashioned from knowledge and imagination. Strengthening and flexing imaginative muscle is perhaps one of the most challenging tasks in many organizations today, largely because organizations are currently designed to put responsibility for that imaginative muscle flexing (or the expectation of it) on those at "the top." Developing a transformative mind and skill set throughout our organizations, as a regular way of doing business, seems an apt gateway to unleashing people's capacity to contribute all of who they are and what they know to meeting the organization's purpose—and, as, Gershon suggests, multiply one another's intelligences. The result is an organization that pulls people upward in the process of working together toward a collectively determined greater good.[17]

In his article "Relational Leading, Neurons, and Grandmothers," Allen Moore provides more food for thought on building and capitalizing on the power of leadership that can come from anywhere in an organizations.

> In my work as a consultant, I am often asked to engage with an organization to "help improve their leadership". Entering the engagement, I am tempted to ask just exactly where do they think their leadership exists. Is it locked away in a cabinet drawer? Following sparseness theory, do they assume that leadership resides only in a few critical senior executive neurons at corporate

headquarters? As one who chooses a relational perspective, I'm much more biased toward a distributed representation camp. Leadership is far too wondrously complex to fit into a model labeled sparseness; it is much more than the sum of individual leaders. Viewing leadership as distributed throughout the organization, an abundant set of dynamic relationships emerges. This capacity is observed as the organization's ability to make sense of environmental challenges or opportunities, to invoke shared practices, and to continually learn and adapt toward a shared purpose. When this capacity is reduced, there are a few areas the practitioner can seek to strengthen: the webs of relationships, the emphasis on community, and clarification of shared purpose, the quality of dialog, the adoption of shared practices, and the courage to iterate forward into the unknown. Relational theory, grandmothers and neurons all support an understanding that knowing exists in relating.[18]

Distributed leadership and internal accountability go hand in hand in our educational systems as we work together in a transformative change process. My line of thinking here goes as follows: if school community members see their reflection in the values, purposes, and vision for the organization, then the likelihood of their capacity to "own" the organization and bring more of who they are and what they believe they can become to the change process increases exponentially. Embedded in that ownership is a drive for results. When we truly own something (see ourselves as responsible for its current state of being), we are far less likely to be willing to see it fail. Problems are viewed not as barriers but as opportunities to creatively tap more of the system capacity in discovering what actions can be taken to get to the results we want. Leadership of that process is not a linear relationship. In multiple supportive ways, everyone manages everyone, because everyone is invested in the success of the enterprise.

Conversely, when we are mandated to perform and see no reflection of ourselves in the decisions or change program being "handed down," then we are far more prone to not only resist but quite possibly work to defeat the effort.

In the next section, we find how AI can offer dramatic support to building the quality of partnering we see in high internal accountability systems.

## APPRECIATIVE INQUIRY—A MODEL FOR SOCIAL AND ORGANIZATIONAL CHANGE

*When the music changes, so does the dance.*
—African proverb

Since its development in the late '80s as both a theory and methodology for knowledge creation and utilization, AI has taken the world of organizational change by storm. Across the globe, large groups—from hundreds to thousands—are engaging with the principles and practices of AI to bring new life to their ways of organizing and enabling their success in fulfilling Mahatma Gandhi's charge to "be the kind of change you want to see in the world." The positive resonance AI has had for so many so quickly can perhaps be summed up by this quote from Victor Hugo: "Nothing is so powerful as an idea whose time has come."

As Ken Gergen, the author of "Toward Generative Theory," puts it: "The growth and application of AI over the past two decades has been nothing short of phenomenal. It is arguably the most powerful process of positive organizational change ever devised."[19]

**Principles and Practices of Appreciative Inquiry**

First and foremost, AI is well known for how it differs from the traditional problem-solving approach to change. An AI mantra might be, "what gives life, matters." Organizations and groups are viewed as having innumerable strengths and assets that can be revealed through inquiry. In contrast, the traditional problem-solving approach can be likened to a more medical model where organizations are seen as problems to be diagnosed, treated, and solved. Whitney and Trosten-Bloom highlight these differences in the table below.[20]

| | Deficit-Based Change | Positive Change |
|---|---|---|
| Intervention focus | Identified problem | Affirmative topics |
| Participation | Selective inclusion of people | Whole system |
| Action Research | Diagnosis of problem<br>Causes and consequences<br>Quantitative analysis<br>Profile of need<br>Conducted by outsiders | Discovery of positive core<br>Organization at its best<br>Narrative analysis<br>Map of positive core<br>Conducted by members |
| Dissemination | Feedback to decision makers | Widespread and creative sharing of best practices |
| Creative potential | Brainstormed list of alternatives | Dreams of a better world and the organization's contribution |
| Result | Best solution to resolve the problem | Design to realize dreams and human aspirations |
| Capacity gained | Capacity to implement and measure the plan | Capacity for ongoing positive change |

Public educators can likely call up multiple examples of change efforts that have been introduced using a deficit frame. Decreasing bullying, reducing drop-out rate, and closing the achievement gap are but a few. What goes hand in hand with identifying what's not working is usually blame and shame—and a review of the past to find the culprits or cause. Looking out the rearview mirror in this vein is not a strategy for growth—it is a strategy for hindering relationships. My experience has been that when we're seeking blame or negative cause, people spend more time looking to avoid being the source of the problem than trying to be the source of possibility.

In her book *Positive Psychology at Work* Sarah Lewis discusses the five principles that underpin the shift in the approach to organizational change that AI represents. I've drawn from her descriptions and added words in italics commonly used to summarize each principle:

The **anticipatory principle** is about the power of imagination to pull systems toward attractive futures. When we create a picture of the future that is imbued with our energy, aspiration and hope, we are drawn to do things that make the realization of that future more likely. It refers to the inspiring and directing effect of a powerful dream. *Images inspire action.*

The **positive principle** refers to the power of positive emotional energy to sustain change. Fredrickson's work is increasingly demonstrating the capabilities, capacities, and energy created and released by people, and particularly groups, when experiencing positive emotions. *Positive affect effects change.*

The **constructionist principle** reflects the importance given to the joint making of meaning. This is a reflection of the understanding of the organization as a complex adaptive system, created and enacted by those within it. It is based on the understanding of the social world as being socially and collectively constructed by those that form it. *Words create worlds.*

The **simultaneity principle** encapsulates the idea that things happen together: to change a pattern of relating is to change the system. This reflects a complex adaptive system understanding of organizations with its patterns of recursive dynamics. *Inquiry creates change.*

The **poetic principle** notes that an organization is a living human system where communication and conversation are the fabric of the organization. *We can choose what we study.* [21]

These principles are embedded in the process of AI, known as the 4-D cycle:[22]

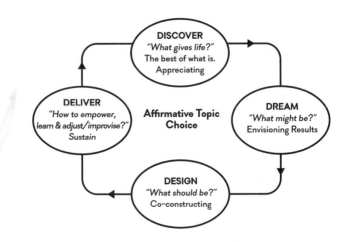

Figure 2.1  **4-D MODEL OF APPRECIATIVE INQUIRY**

Cooperrider and Whitney provide detail on this model:

*Discovery*—Mobilizing the whole system by engaging all stakeholders in the articulation of strengths and best practices. Identifying "The best of what has been and what is."

*Dream*—Creating a clear results-oriented vision in relation to discovered potential and in relation to questions of higher purpose, such as, "What is the world calling us to become?"

*Design*—Creating possibility propositions of the ideal organization, articulating an organization design that people feel capable of drawing upon and magnifying the positive core to realize the newly expressed dream.

*Destiny*—Strengthening the affirmative capability of the whole system, enabling it to build hope and sustain momentum for ongoing positive change and high performance. Engaging in the work necessary to implement positive changes and foster ongoing, generative conversations for change.[23]

In the context of AI, consider the weighty importance of choosing the affirmative topic: if inquiry and change are a simultaneous moment; if the questions we ask set the stage for what we find; if what we discover (the data) creates the material out of which the future is conceived, conversed about, and constructed; then, what we inquire into matters deeply. Samples of affirmative topics that have relevance for education are presented below, contrasted to those that might emerge from a problem-oriented focus:

- Extraordinary student engagement in learning (versus increasing poor test scores)

- Excellence in meeting the variable learning needs of each and every child (versus changing from whole group teaching)

- High staff commitment and sense of shared ownership (versus improvement of low morale)

- A magnetic work environment (versus decreasing high turnover)

- A powerful and supportive student community (versus decreasing disciplinary referrals)

- An inclusive community devoted to social justice for all (versus eliminating marginalization of students of color and those with disabilities)

It is important to note that because of the generative nature of the AI process, not all change agendas might dictate use of the AI process specifically as it's outlined in the 4-D model. In fact, that would be contradictory to the generative theory embedded in AI. Your decisions about how to use AI practices will be fashioned by the change agenda you are looking to address (e.g., organizational change, interorganizational planning, team development, community development, etc.), the type of engagement that's most appropriate to your context (e.g., whole system 4-D dialogue, AI summit, AI learning team, etc.) and resources that are available to you.[24] One of the most widely used AI forms of engagement is the large-scale AI summit. In their book *The Appreciative Inquiry Summit: A Practitioner's Guide for Leading Large-Group Change*, James Ludema, et.al, situate this methodology alongside many other whole-system approaches that emerged in the 1980s but distinguish the AI summit as being particularly important in today's world:

The AI Summit is based on the understanding that the future is truly unknown and unknowable, and that people in organizations are continuously involved in the process of building something new. When they are most alive and vital, they are not simply improving systems, they are jointly inventing surprising new ways of organizing. This perspective is particularly important in today's world, in which vigorous global competition, instantaneous electronic communication, and the elimination of political, cultural, and geographic boundaries are rapidly re-configuring the social and economic landscape.[25]

AI summit methodology is a part of the newest evolution in thought on managing change. It makes a particular contribution because of its emphasis on the power of the positive to unleash extraordinary performance, and how that positivity influences the relational field essential for innovating, as reflected in the table below.[26]

| 1900 | 1950 | 1965 | 1980s | 2000+ |
|------|------|------|-------|-------|
| Experts solve specific problems | Everyone solves specific problems | Experts improve whole systems | Everyone improves whole systems | Everyone innovates for extraordinary performance |

In the exercises section of the book you will find an example of a district level organizational change summit. In the resources section, information is provided for organizational change summits in other educational contexts.

## GENERATIVITY PLUS POSITIVITY EQUAL TRANSFORMATIVE CHANGE

Much has been written since the onset of AI about the importance of emphasizing the positive. From my experience carrying this work into the world, the introduction of the positive principle has garnered much receptivity as well as some suspicion or pushback. The erroneous perception that AI ignores problems is the predominant criticism. It is my guess that this is rooted in some applications of AI not reflecting fidelity to the importance of both positivity and generativity in AI theory and practice. Positivity is seductive when in fact it may be that generativity is the heavier weighted variable necessary for creating transformative change. To help distinguish what is meant by *generativity*, consider the definitions below.

1. Merriam-Webster defines *generative* as "relating to or capable of production or reproduction" as in "the generative power of the life force."

2. On generativity and AI, Cooperrider notes:

In its most pragmatic form AI represents a data-based theory building methodology for evolving and putting into practice the collective will of an organization. It has one and only one aim—to provide a generative theoretical springboard for normative dialogue that is conducive to self-directed experimentation in social innovation.[27]

3. Gervase R. Bushe summarizes generativity as "the processes and capacities that help people see old things in new ways."[28] He goes on to say: "Generativity occurs when a group of people discover, create, and/or are presented with an image that allows them to experience their work and

organization differently. A generative image allows people to see the world anew, identify new options, formulate new strategies, even reform their identity. The most generative images influence our feelings and motivations as well as our thoughts. People want to take new decisions and actions because of how attractive that image is." Bushe depicts this in the figure below (from Bushe, 2013).[29]

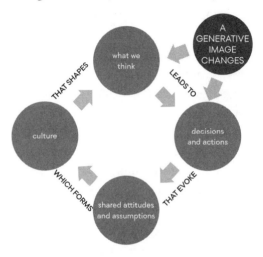

**Fig. 2.2  HOW GENERATIVITY CHANGES ORGANIZATIONS**

In knitting this thinking on generativity together, it seems clear that positivity alone is insufficient to stimulate traveling along the path that Bushe lays out above, and that it is the essential equation of generativity and positivity that contributes to transformative organizational change. Bushe's own earlier writing suggests this as well:

There are many useful ways in which "the positive" can help create OD (organizational development) interventions that are more generative, and support the process of change in general . . . how positive emotions, the ratio of positive to negative talk, positive stories, hope, the power from having a positive attitude, and focusing on what you want more of (not what you want less of) can be used in the service of transformational change.[30]

In a generative frame, curiosity and learning conversations reign. If our intention is to innovate and grow, then we must expand, not narrow, the relational flow between individuals and groups to allow for and nourish multiple perspectives and explore multiple realities in our inquiry, design, decision-making, and action planning. We need to create within our organizations and ourselves a context for leading change that can occur as a matter of course out of how we are being with one another. A context that compels us to behave with one another in ways that make visible our trust, respect, and value for freedom of expression—and has us mine for the gold each person has to offer. That gold can be found, too, in the why underpinning an individual's or group's cynicism or resistance to change. The role of inquiry in AI is not limited to the positive, as might be misinterpreted by many. If we are venturing to bring everyone into the conversation to plan and innovate for change, then facilitating productive ways to unpack the cynical perspective opens a wellspring of possibility. Judgment and a critical nature shut down inquiry (and generative potential) and limit the possibility we can reap from our relationships. Exercising compassion and skill at unearthing the deeper "why" that fuels cynicism and exploring what the unrealized dreams are in those conversations can strengthen relationships and the relational flow of information and knowledge that can be useful to creating new opportunities and positive results, actions that benefit the organizational entity and/or movement.

Conversely, marginalizing people whom we find difficult to communicate with and/or who are not perceived to be readily coming forward with support for a change agenda may translate into a loss of innovative capacity. In addition, the mere act of listening from a place of unadulterated curiosity can have the synergistic effect of amplifying the speaker's strengths and knowledge that were heretofore unrecognized—cloaked by fear of judgment or retaliation. All combined, a positive approach to the articulation of that which is not working, perceived as unworkable, or ostensibly undesired. Otherwise said, light from darkness, all voices matter.

Innovators know well the power of idea generation in creating breakthroughs in design and the essential importance of being vigilant in their practice to avoid the danger of squelching or marginalizing perspectives. IDEO, one of the top design firms in the world, manifests this belief. Generativity and positivity are at the core of their success. Design thinking and practice are increasingly influencing progress in areas beyond product and structural design, including societal responsibilities such as health and education.

As evidenced in our own six-sphere framework for appreciative organizing, I think there is clear opportunity for transforming our public schools by focusing and nurturing the power of generativity and positivity to bring out the best in each other, and building organizational environments of mutual learning and support.

## APPRECIATIVE ORGANIZING

*Not only do people want their own lives to be full of meaning and purpose, but they also expect the same of their organizations.*
—Diana Whitney

Organizations that emanate life are compelling. A community of people organizing together in service of a shared vision has power. They inspire and energize. There is overt recognition for the value of collective effort and each individual's contribution. Reflect for a moment on an organization or organized effort that you've experienced as being full of life. Perhaps a professional project in your school district or a faith-based or civic organization to which you have contributed. Diana Whitney offers principles of appreciative organizing that help us create positive change in our school community. The foundation that Whitney builds on is this: there is life in everything, and we can consciously, individually and collectively, make a difference in creating or depleting that life. I briefly summarize below Whitney's nine principles for appreciative organizing.[31]

## 1. Evolutionary Purpose

"An evolutionary purpose ensures that life will continue and thrive—physically, mentally, emotionally and spiritually into the future."[32] It is our ideal future, representative of the stand that we take based on our collective commitment. An evolutionary purpose looks forward and pulls us upward.

## 2. Harmonious Wholeness

"Wholeness brings out the best of people. By drawing on diverse ideas and aligning strengths it creates one harmonious direction forward."[33] Fundamental to this principle is the acknowledgment of our connectedness, not our separateness. It relates not only to our wholeness as organizations but as individuals, deeply recognizing that we cannot bifurcate our personal and professional selves. Embedded is a holistic view of being human, and valuing the integration of our head, heart, and hands in all that we choose to do. Choices guided by a vision or purpose that binds us together and is bigger than any one of us.

## 3. Appreciative Leadership

Leadership that gives voice to people throughout the organization and that values everyone's ideas and opinions.[34] Talking at people puts them to sleep or invites them to resist. Talking with them awakens the spirit of possibility and generates a lively organizational environment. Listening to them evokes deep knowing and builds relational commitment needed for extraordinary results to unfold. Appreciative leaders foster conversations that matter.[35]

### 4. Positive Emotional Climate

The operative words here are *safety* and *trust*—manifest in the freedom we feel to self-express. When we feel safe in our organizations, made possible by an experience of trust, then we freely express our thoughts, feelings, ideas, and make obvious by the ways we speak and listen to one another that we value the self-expression of others. This fosters a climate of openness that is fertile ground for creativity and collaboration.

### 5. Strong Centers of Meaning

"Strong centers of meaning are more often socially negotiated and determined than assigned."[36] At its core this principle refers to individuals having a role in authoring and enacting how the future is created. This is heavily linked to a positive emotional climate and is the fuel for collaboration and shared responsibility. This is co-construction versus command and control and welcoming multiple perspectives versus a single and dictated "right" way.

### 6. Just in Time Structures

Three significant themes are articulated in this principle:
- From hierarchical to distributed
- From assigned role to the continuous alignment of strengths
- From clock time to relational time[37]

Each of these themes relates to the capacity we have to be adaptable via the organizational structures that we create. If "structure" looks to us like one single way of doing things—then in the current global climate, we're at risk for being dinosaurs. On the other hand, if our "structures" are imbued with fluidity, based on aligning and expanding strengths for the tasks at hand and respecting individuals as whole human beings who seek meaning and fulfillment in their work—then those structures support and reflect adaptability and flexibility. Adhocracy and/or holacracy, rather than bureaucracy, are favored as a means to foster the engagement of organizational members and be responsive to the new knowledge they are continually generating and the actions they determine are the "best fit" in response to that new knowledge.

## 7. Liberation Economics

Whitney's own words here best serve our understanding of this principle:

> Imagine instead, economic policies and practices designed to enable access to education and healthcare for all. Imagine an economic system designed to create a balance of autonomy and collective social justice across the globe. Imagine an economic process that fostered collaboration among people who themselves felt cared for and confident to contribute to the good of the whole. It is not only possible, it is essential, to design economic systems through a positive, life giving lens.[38]

## 8. Engaged Participation

Inclusivity, self-organization, and a "cohering center" (as opposed to a top-down hierarchal image) are paramount in this principle. Engaged participation is premised on the belief that we can contribute to "life" in our organizations when members have an authentic voice in the decisions that affect them; are given autonomy to self-manage their work; and when the formal leadership serves as the central support for messaging how all the moving parts work together in service to the shared vision.

### 9. Caring Culture

"When people are cared for they have energy and effort to care for others. When leaders, managers and supervisors care for people those people learn to care for others."[39]

A caring culture is manifest in our communication and the visible ways in which we relate to one another as human beings. It is shown in the shifts we make from punitive forms of evaluation to support for growth and success; from the aforementioned dual perspective of professional and personal to appreciation of and respect for our wholeness as human beings; and from a focus solely on results to being mindful of what's needed to create a context in which sustainable, positive change can occur, paying attention to each of the other principles of appreciative organizing.

## FROM PATHOLOGY TO POSSIBILITY

The groundbreaking work of AI has influenced and/or run simultaneous with corollary strengths-based, positively oriented theoretical and practical developments in the fields of psychology, education, social work, organizational design, leadership, ecology, economics, and conflict resolution. This growing body of work, as it relates to organizational life, is represented in *Positive Organizational Scholarship: Foundations of a New Discipline*, edited by Cameron, Dutton, and Quinn[40] and *The Oxford Handbook of Positive Organizational Scholarship*, edited by Cameron and Spreitzer.[41]

Positive Organizational Scholarship (POS) is an umbrella concept used to emphasize what elevates and what is inspiring to individuals and organizations by defining and improving on the challenging, broken, and needlessly difficult. Just as positive psychology explores optimal individual psychological states rather than pathological ones, POS focuses attention on the generative dynamics in organizations that lead to the development of human strength, foster resiliency in employees, enable healing and restoration, and cultivate extraordinary individual and organizational performance. While POS does not ignore dysfunctional or typical patterns of behavior, it is most interested in the motivations and effects associated with remarkably positive phenomena—how they are facilitated, why they work, how they can be identified, and how organizations can capitalize on them.[42]

It is largely from POS that we have sourced our thinking about ways to support and elevate positive transformative narratives within America's public schools. Changing our lens from pathology to possibility in organizational life is integrally woven with our commitment to do the same in our personal lives.

### The SOAR Framework

As a direct outgrowth of AI and positive organizational scholarship, Leonard and I have found the SOAR framework (Strengths, Opportunities, Aspirations, and Results) to be user friendly to educational stakeholders. It can be employed as an advanced organizer in small group work and larger scale engagements. Critical to the success of SOAR implementation is keeping fidelity to the tenet of whole system engagement and representation.

Below, two graphics help to define and illustrate the SOAR framework, including how it differs from another well-known strategic planning framework called SWOT (Strengths, Weaknesses, Opportunities, and Threats). A major intent to be gleaned from SOAR is to move away from the need to elicit "buy-in" from stakeholders after strategic decisions are made that affect them—and toward building early stakeholder ownership of strategic decisions by engaging them in the process of making them.[43]

Transformation into SOAR

| Strategic Inquiry | Strengths | Opportunities |
|---|---|---|
| | What are we doing well? What are our greatest assets? | What are the best possible market opportunities? How do we best partner with others? |
| Appreciative Intent | Aspirations | Results |
| | To what do we aspire? What is our preferred future? | What do we want to be known for? What are our measurable cresults? |

| SWOT-Analysis | SOAR-Framework |
|---|---|
| Equal focus on Weaknesses and Threats | Focus on Strengths and Opportunities |
| Competition focus – "just be better" | Potential focus – " be the best possible" |
| Incremental improvement | Innovation and value generation |
| Top down | Stakeholder engagement |
| Focus on analysis and planning | Focus on planning and implementation |
| Energy depleting | Energy creating |
| Attention to gaps | Attention to results |

Permission to use from Stavros, J. & Hinrichs, G. (2009). The Thin Book of SOAR: Building Strengths-Based Strategy (Bend, OR: Thin Book Publishing), 11–12. www.thinbook.com.

In an example from education, Cooperrider and Godwin incorporated SOAR into the framework for an AI design summit they facilitated in Houston, Texas, in 2009 called "Healthy Kids—Healthy Schools." The following link provides additional information on materials they used in their summit as well as video highlights of the event: http://www.taosinstitute.net/healthy-kids-healthy-schools.[44]

## SHIFTS IN THINKING, BEING, AND DOING IN ORGANIZATIONAL LIFE—IT STARTS WITH SELF

Coming full circle, I revisit the organizing question that served as the stimulus for this chapter: "What is the world asking of organizations now that is different from how we have designed organizational models and ways of organizing in the past?" I'll start by putting up onto the marquee a short list of the dominant themes represented in the research and experience of the authors and practitioners whose perspectives, theories, and practices relating to organizational change and ways of organizing I've addressed.

1. Self-awareness—subjugating ego

2. Self as the source of possibility, personal responsibility, and integrity

3. Transcendent core purpose

4. Future orientation

5. Positivity, generativity, and relational flow

6. Identifying, aligning, and leveraging strengths —individual and system

7. Autonomy, self-management (leading from any chair)

8. Productive conflict engagement

9. Responsibility for the other, empathy, caring, compassion

10. Wholeness, individual (personal and professional), system (cooperative capacity), and planet (nature and the global community)

11. Inclusion rather than exclusion

Acknowledging the vastness of possibility that these life-centric themes offer us in shaping our organizational lives might be both exciting and somewhat daunting. Adopting a transformative approach to change aligned with the short list above seems to squarely and ultimately rest on our willingness to commit to and take ownership for our individual self-awareness and growth, to expand exponentially our generosity of thought, compassion, humility, and overall humanity, and to fully wake up to recognizing and valuing how we are being in the world largely determines how the world will be. This type of growth is vertical development. It's a deepening of our understanding of ourselves, expanding our consciousness and personal capacity to be more comfortable with the ambiguity and complexity of the world. Thinking back to Laloux, owning that the more conscious we are, the more possibilities we can see for ourselves and others to adapt in collectively configuring ways to realize our purpose and increase our joint aliveness in the process.

While writing this chapter, I read a small but powerful book, *Getting to Yes with Yourself* by William Ury, cofounder of Harvard's Program on Negotiation. Ury is known worldwide for his work on negotiation.[45] He opens with this quote from Socrates: "Let him who would move the world first move himself."[46] Two passages from Ury's book expand on this message:

> Getting to yes with ourselves brings a larger and more generous perspective that benefits everyone around us and makes possible not only a win with others, but a third win for the larger whole. The work on ourselves inspires us to imagine and to work toward a world in which every single human being matters.

> I have devoted much of my professional life to trying to prevent and stop wars. Peace is my passion. If someone had told me thirty-five years ago that the key to peace was inner peace, I would have thought them utopian and unrealistic. I preferred instead to work on something more practical—which was to focus on strategies for negotiation. Now I have come to realize that I was the one who was perhaps unrealistic in believing that we

could arrive at a sustained peace in the world without also doing the necessary work within ourselves.[47]

Bob Anderson, founder and CEO of the Leadership Circle, echoes Ury's emphasis on the deep personal growth that is essential to effecting change.

The critical flaw in the way that most organizational change efforts are constructed is that they pay too little attention to the deep personal changes that are required of people at every level. The flawed assumption is that we can create the new culture out of the level of consciousness, thinking, and behavior that gave rise to the old culture. When this fatal flaw remains unchallenged the change efforts start with a flurry of energy, vision, and activity; only to grind to a halt when people start waiting for others to change first and to give them permission to act on a new vision. This disempowered stance blocks substantial personal and organization change from taking place.

When this type of thinking is prevalent in a system, meaningful change is nearly impossible because there is not enough individual leadership present to get anything moving. Leadership happens when one of us (at any level) decides that what is going on around us is our responsibility, that the success of the business, and our life, is in our own hands. And that we need wait for no one to begin creating the future we want.[48]

Consider the sage words of Ury and Anderson and my short list of themes in reflecting on the strengths in your work and organizational life. It would be surprising to learn that there is much presented in this chapter that is not already something you know intellectually and intuitively about what fuels your own positive dispositions: optimism, hopefulness, resilience, and your capacity to create, in collaboration with others, positive sustainable change. What may not be readily apparent is how to orchestrate more of it, particularly in the current context of America's public school system.

## IMAGINING POSSIBILITIES FOR APPRECIATIVE ORGANIZING IN PUBLIC EDUCATION

Perhaps the way to begin imagining possibilities is to ask two fundamental questions: Why do we educate our children? Why do individuals choose to become educators, particularly public school educators? If I were to get a group of educators together for such an interview, I'd likely hear deeply moving stories describing the desire to play a significant role in supporting children to thrive as human beings, to flourish in communities, to find meaning and accomplishment in life, to feel good about themselves and as a result have a greater capacity to feel good about the world with all its complexity and uncertainty. And that would be the tip of the iceberg.

Similarly, I imagine that most public school educators might have chosen their path in part because of the inclusionary aspect of "public"—schools for each and every child, not just some. They might share stories about public school educators who contributed to their lives and how their influence fueled their desire to give back some of what was given to them. Perhaps they envisioned being public school educators as an opportunity to join with other people who share their desire to help shape a society through its young people. And that what they want for their students is the same thing that they want for themselves—to feel like they are making a difference in bettering the world at large. I invite you to ask these questions in your own school communities as a means to discover the positive core of your system via the stories that your colleagues tell. The results could be a building block in imagining the future.

## FOUR QUESTIONS

I close this chapter with four questions to help stimulate additional thinking about ways to strengthen the appreciative fabric of American public schools.

1. How can we emphasize drivers for public school transformation that are aligned with positive organizational scholarship?

2. How can we use whole system engagement to unleash capacity?

3. How can we nurture our appreciative capacities and that of others?

4. How can we increase progressive interactions and render regressive resistance irrelevant?

### Appreciative Drivers for Public School Change

Building off of the work of Michael Fullan in his article "Choosing the Wrong Drivers for Whole System Reform,"[49] I concur that an investment in capacity building and group quality and a systemic mind-set are superior drivers for change than a sole focus on individual quality, a data system that tracks student achievement and technology. The latter are useful and not to be ignored, however, they should not be the engines running the train. In this chapter we have seen a glimpse of how an investment in personal awareness and growth, collaborative practices, engagement, and trust building can fuel group quality. It's possible to embed teacher appraisal in a school culture of learning (students, families, and educators alike) where individuals are genuinely motivated from the feedback they receive—and where strategies are employed that leverage the group, rather than pit people against each another in a competitive vein.

We can initiate this work by asking affirmative questions of our school community that help us to identify the current strengths within the system. We can spend time creating and committing to a positive image of the future that is aligned with the values people in the system hold for equity and excellence for each and every child. We can use that future view (and the transcendent core purpose it represents) to be lovingly ruthless about what is essential to accomplishing it. We can use it, too, to create coherence, communication, and coordination between all the moving parts in the system. As suggested earlier in this chapter, this may be the role that formal leadership plays in a distributed leadership system—that of a "cohering center."

### Living Dangerously and Sustainably—Whole System Engagement

When we marginalize the opposition, when we assume we know what people are thinking and what they are capable of, when we compartmentalize and fragment our roles, responsibilities, and interactions, we seriously delimit the capacity of our systems. If we believe that our systems are full of positive potential waiting to be discovered and unpacked, then the question becomes, "How can we engage in the risk taking necessary to tap that potential?" One response would be to structure whole system engagement on an affirmative, generative topic, versus limiting the inquiry or engagement to a small group representing various constituencies. There are multiple examples in the literature of large group summits fostering transformative change at a speed atypically associated with change processes that could serve as models for what we can do in our own school communities.

While whole-system engagement calls for a commitment to appreciative, relational leadership, it calls too for reflection on our individual relationship with hope and our beliefs about humanity.

As Ury might offer, can we say yes to life? And if so, can it bolster us in opening up our inquiry to more than just those people who live within the walls or close surrounds of our school communities? What's the possibility of increasing our connectedness to all our public school stakeholders and making them an integral part of our visioning and strategic planning? If our modus operandi is, as Brené Brown writes, "Keep everyone at a safe distance and always have an exit strategy,"[50] then whole system engagement would look less possible. In contrast, if we deepen our personal growth and use that knowledge to hone our skills in productive conflict engagement, then we can expand our personal capacity to enlarge the circle of who is engaged in the conversation about transformation and innovation.

## Nurturing Appreciative Capacities

Perhaps the most fitting tool in nurturing our appreciative capacities is to be diligently mindful of the questions we ask. "What you place your attention on grows" is a saying that seems to be out there but not attributable to any one person. Certainly it's a bedrock principle of AI. What you inquire into determines what you find. In the hugely diverse universe of public schools in America, it excites me to think about what we might find if we consciously invest in an inquiry into the positive core of our public schools. We've begun that inquiry in this book and in the afterword we discuss some future steps for deepening and broadening the process.

## Fostering Progressive Interactions

When John, Leonard, and I began discussing the application of AI to public education, I revisited Michael Fullan's book *Leadership and Sustainability*. Interestingly, Fullan titles the epilogue "It's Going to Be Hard." His explanation is essentially rooted in a belief that the reality that we face in public schools is one where more people are wired to notice what's wrong—what's not working (regressive interactions)—versus what's needed (progressive interactions). He suggests "progressive interactions" are requisite to achieve systems thinkers who can lead continual system change, capacity building, and sustainability. He asserts that regressive interactions diminish the much needed system or organizational intelligence but proliferate because they are easier.[51]

That was the "hook" that we as a writing team used to move us forward to write this book with a focus on public schools. I see positive strengths-based change and positive organizational scholarship on the whole as directly contributing to the paradigmatic shift needed to increase "progressive interactions" among all stakeholders for public schooling in America. Combined, they offer applicable knowledge and tools that can be used to transform the way we work together across the educational system—school, district, state, federal, and larger stakeholder communities. They can contribute to positive growth, innovation, and sustainability, perhaps at a faster pace than normally thought possible given the resonance appreciative organizing holds for what people really want in our public schools—and in life. I am hopeful that you can imagine even more possibilities for what can be.

# CHAPTER THREE
## The Third Sphere of AO
### Relational Leadership
John L. Mann

*You don't try to make people think or feel in any particular way. Instead, you try to get them to be themselves. Art doesn't try to dictate what you think. It helps you change yourself.*[1]
—Keith Oatley and Maja Djikic

Two principals attend the same district briefing at the central administration office. On the drive back to school both leaders have questions about the new proposal their boss is pushing. *How do I handle this new initiative on top of tomorrow's challenges? What steps do I take to be effective and efficient? Do I ask for more time? Do I plead for a delay in the initiative's introduction given all the things we have going on in the building? Do I simply tell the staff that we have to deal with it and do what the district wants? How do I sell the initiative without selling out the district command and without compromising my staff and sapping their energy away from current projects? How do I please everyone?*

This dilemma is not unique in our time of rapid change and calls for increased student performance. Vast quantities of Diet Coke and cold pizza have been consumed puzzling over answers to these questions. I confronted similar demands while serving as a principal for twenty-one years and a district leadership development director for eight years in Pasco County, Florida. I hear similar concerns in my current role as a principal trainer at the University of South Florida. At USF, I was introduced to Appreciative Inquiry as part of the work Linda, Leonard, and I did with six counties surrounding Tampa. My AI training reaffirmed my long-held belief in the power and the importance of other people's strengths and the potential that lies in people, not programs or data. Relational leadership is the fundamental starting point for leadership to flourish. It is the key to organizational success and increased personal fulfillment for leaders in schools and school districts.

We are being challenged to adapt to an ever-changing world monthly if not weekly or daily. It is a world bent on imposing a premium on a "break and fix" mentality instead of focusing on "strengths and improvement" toward the purposes and values we hold most dear. What are the things that will stand the test of time? Will our actions and decisions matter twenty years from today?

Relational leadership is foundational to our argument that appreciative organizing in public education starts the process of developing purpose and core values, and it evolves as the organization adds frontline leaders to continuously improve schools and school districts. The challenges of unstable environments should not be wrestled to the ground to determine dominance but should provide an opportunity to practice how a symbiotic relationship between positive attributes and an expansion of strengths wins the day. Such steady leadership is tested as state legislatures attempt to reform education annually. Rarely does a state-initiated improvement plan ask you to identify what you are doing right. Almost 100 percent of the time, it focuses on how bad you are at closing academic achievement gaps, handling behavior, or raising graduation and college enrollment rates. States are always asking schools and districts to create goals and improvement plans in a mandated area with the hope of getting back to a zero baseline. That sounds reasonable, but the lack of progress being made is very clear. This approach is not working well. No Child Left Behind (NCLB) did require data on all subgroups of students to uncover their need for support and reaffirmed the importance of qualified, subject-specific teachers. But achievement gaps remain today and in some cases have grown larger not smaller since the inception of NCLB.

It is time to work toward a desired future through a strength-based approach. Work from your strengths for the greatest opportunity for success. The relational leader needs to clearly understand the challenges and negotiate the impact of external forces on the internal accountability structure and processes of the school or district. The relational leader garners public and private support by designing ways to increase the well-being of all children.

## WHAT IS RELATIONAL LEADERSHIP?

In my personal dictionary under the entry for *relational leaders* I have a small group of pictures. Max Ramos's snapshot is in a special place. Over twenty-five years ago Max hired me as an assistant principal at Hudson Middle School. Every day Max worked to create a culture of trust, caring, and respect. I became an experienced district and state trainer because he believed in me and gave me opportunities to stretch my wings. I learned the importance of staff, student, and parent relations in establishing a well-grounded school. In the book *Relational Leading: Practices for Dialogically Based Collaboration*, Lone Hersted and Kenneth Gergen define relational leading as "the ability of persons in relationships to move with engagement and efficacy into the future. In this sense, relational leading is an activity, not a personal trait."[2] Attributes that best inform relational leading start with understanding that vitality is dependent on the flow of dialogue characterized by "collaboration, empowerment, horizontal decision-making, information sharing, networking, continuous learning, appreciation and connectivity. It continues by placing a premium on truth, trust and respect. Synching your actions and your words is imperative as you consistently build teams to enhance performance and viability."[3] A veteran employee shared with me that after many years and many principal changes, he admired Max for his truthful and respectful approach. This is the type of impact that school leaders must strive for. Carolyn Shields, a champion of the importance of moral dialogue and its inclusivity, writes,

> I suggest that transformative educational leaders may foster the academic success of all children through engaging in moral dialogue that facilitates the development of strong relationships, supplants pathologizing silences, challenges existing beliefs and practices, and grounds educational leadership in some criteria for social justice.[4]

I have come to believe what Leslie Tucker of Roundstone International has argued. Without fulfilling the demands of "the relational field," which include establishing trust and respect as well as the freedom to express oneself while establishing common commitment to the work envisioned or desired, the leader will never create the necessary and sufficient conditions to get the desired results. Tucker calls this first and most crucial stage of implementation of any significant innovation "the foundation for results."[5]

## BUILDING RELATIONAL CAPITAL THROUGH DISPOSITIONS

Relational leaders are both marathoners and sprinters. As marathoners, they start the journey thinking about their legacy. Relational leaders willingly and freely help their neighboring districts, schools, or departments. They care more about the overall success of everyone than that their help will not be recognized and their district, school, or department might not gain a competitive edge. They care deeply about results but not at the expense of people. They work to establish a culture of high expectations with a laser focus supported by hard work and layered with positive energy.

As sprinters, they move quickly to meet the many demands of students, staff, parents, and others, grounded in their core purpose and values. The relational leader chooses to take action in both the short and long term with the well-being of others as their inspiration. Modeling positive interactions and sharing stories of hope based upon strengths are pivotal in creating an environment of success. An attitude of persistence dedicated to inquiry and action supports the tenets of relational leadership through thick and thin.

The definition of relational leadership becomes clearer then: a relational leader in an appreciative organization develops relational capital while being goal oriented, tenacious, resilient, and purposeful. Relational leaders build leadership organizational capacity on a foundation of relational capital. Relational capital is illustrated as leaders demonstrate the dispositions of high levels of caring, being respectful and trustworthy, maintaining their passion, instilling hope, and being grateful and kind (as depicted in figure 3.1).

Doing the right things for all stakeholders creates relational capital. From teachers to bus drivers, the goal is the freedom to act with integrity and to pursue the purpose with all your talent and passion. Relational capital is key to developing an individual's, team's, or organization's relational net worth. It is the reservoir of all the strengths and assets the community has acquired over time by working collaboratively toward its purposes and goals.

Being a relational leader and doing the work that relational leaders do furthers our development and maximizes relational capital. We start first by searching out how success stories, accompanied by important actions, can change the direction of an organization. Each person needs to consider whether they are fulfilled and connected when they go home at the end of the day. Are you excited about future challenges? Are you recommending that people you care about consider the leadership path you are on because of the meaning and purpose it gives to you? We believe this can be the case if we focus on what makes the most difference, not focusing on just the most legislated things. This is where the journey begins.

## BEING RELATIONAL LEADERS AND DOING RELATIONAL LEADING

Relational leaders are optimistic that they can positively influence the DNA of their school, district, or educational organization. We can discover some interesting ideas and options open to the relational leader with a set of dispositions, knowledge, and skills that truly define them. The excitement of thinking about connecting groups or individual people in meaningful conversations is powerful. It starts with the most powerful questions that we can ask. Whitney et al state, "If you truly wish to change your world, you must change your way of asking questions. It could be that the moment you do so, a totally different world will take shape around you."[6] Sincere, positive observations and strength-based questions expand the realm of possibility so that people feel it is possible to step into the amazing.

As we think about being relational leaders and doing leadership work, it should be noted that relational leadership is never all or nothing. Acknowledging your inner drivers helps establish the type of leader you become and the leadership you provide. Relational leadership is not the quick fix to organizational development. It is much quicker to give an order than to build relational capital. Giving a direct order is necessary when the building is burning down, literally or figuratively. Other than those situations, it is more valuable to utilize your tools to build a transparent and inclusive environment where exploration and growth are encouraged and expected.

The positive effects of relational leadership dispositions are enacted through the communication process focusing on conversations, sharing messages, interpreting dialogue, and the power of questions. Hans-Peter Dachler and Dian-Marie Hosking, in the article "Management and Organization: Relational Perspectives," state, "whether the social process is leadership, management, networking, or negotiation, knowing is an ongoing process of relating."[7] This concept of relating encompasses quality communication in all forms. As we network and build socially constructed realities, we must always acknowledge people's interests and goals.[8] Each point further develops the idea and the complexity of relational leadership. There is a shared responsibility and a social act, which includes nurturing and supporting as a means of influence.[9]

## BUILDING DISPOSITION FOR RELATIONAL LEADERSHIP

The ancient Greeks knew a thing or two about leadership. Aristotle said, "We do not act rightly because we have virtue or excellence, but we rather have those because we have acted rightly. We are what we repeatedly do. Excellence, then, is not an act but a habit." The dispositions—caring, respectful, trustworthy, passionate, hopeful, grateful, and kind—are inner drivers that must become actionable for success. The successful relational leader must develop their relational capital by drawing upon positive dispositions and by developing positive strength-based habits. Developing positive strength-based habits is essential to expanding leadership and organizational capacity. The action steps outlined below always start with relational capital and build leadership and organizational capacity from that foundation.

Dr. Dave Scanga, an assistant superintendent of the District

School Board of Pasco County, was an excellent example of a relational leader. He always considered the implications of his actions on the well-being of the people who might be impacted. The human power of growth and learning, individuality, opportunity, shared mission, vision, core values, power, and influence would not flourish without a deep understanding of the technical aspects. The technical aspects of capacity are political and material resources, structural frameworks, policy and the culture of an organization. The appropriate type of action is very focused but understands the importance of relational capital and the human and technical aspects of the organization. All things will work together for good when set on a good foundation.

## Dispositions of a Relational Leader

Figure 3.1 THE DISPOSITIONS OF A RELATIONAL LEADER

The relationships are further detailed in the chart below illustrating specific dimensions of the capacities and associated actions. Some of the elements of our human and technical dimensions are very clear. Professor of Psychology Daniel Katz argued in 1955 that the skills of effective administrators included both dimensions referenced here and a third, conceptual skills. Others, like culture, clearly can have some technical components, but an equally strong argument might be made for including them under the human dimensions. None of these things are important without the action steps to drive the work. What should not get lost is the place and importance of relational capital as the foundation.

| LEADERSHIP CAPACITY | | ORGANIZATIONAL CAPACITY |
|---|---|---|
| HUMAN | ACTION STEPS | TECHNICAL |
| Growth and learning environment for all | Results | Political structures |
| Opportunity rich environment | Action Orientation | Structural frameworks |
| Shared vision, mission, core values | Laser Focus | Material resources |
| Redistribution of power and influence | Inclusive environment that encourages inquiry and learning | Policy development and management |
| Individuality embraced | Deep understanding of the human and technical aspects of the organization | Culture |
| RELATIONAL CAPITAL | | |

Chart 3.1  HUMAN AND TECHNICAL DIMENSIONS OF CAPACITY BUILDING

## LEVERAGING RELATIONAL CAPITAL

You might leverage your relational capital with a person, team, or organization, but first you must have something to leverage. The action steps must be intentional and be built from the bottom up so relational capital supports both leadership and organizational capacity simultaneously. People who lead through negativity and fear are drawing on an empty account. When they tear down, degrade, order, and humiliate they can get some movement of people and may get some progress on achieving goals. Even though they might make some gains, they are not building anything of substance—no sustainable leadership direction or team. The superintendent who is consistently taking from the relational capital accounts of others will only last until the board changes or until he or she has burned all his or her bridges.

Actively increasing your relational capital is the wise investment that produces dividends over time. The poet Edwin Chapin said it best: "Every action of our lives touches on some chord that will vibrate in eternity." This dynamic impact, created by one person's positive actions, can create an amazing advantage for your organization through accumulated resources. Barbara Fredrickson in her book *Positivity* notes that businessman Marcial Losada believed there is a tipping point where positivity changes the climate—just as there is a tipping point between ice and water. She writes "Losada tracked three dimensions: whether people's statements were (1) positive or negative, (2) self-focused or other-focused, (3) based on inquiry (asking questions) or advocacy (defending a point of view)."[10] Of course, we are all prone to error. Nobody is perfect, right? We all make mistakes, say negative things, or have less than pleasant exchanges. You will be more successful if you keep the balance of scales tipped to the positive side. The problem is that negative statements and deeds have a greater density. Depending upon the speaker, three to six positive statements may be needed to one negative statement to increase the positive advantage. That type of goal will keep us on our toes as we work to become the most positive contributors on our team, department, or school. Jack Zenger writes in the *Forbes* blog:

> The message is this: Focusing on weaknesses will help leaders to be "less bad" in the same way clinical psychology has helped people to be less mentally ill. But no matter how hard you work on curing a weakness it will seldom make the level of impact you could achieve by honing a strength.[11]

Not only do some organizations suffer at the hands of negative leaders, but we are also living in a time when the teaching profession and school leaders are being torn down and devalued by politicians and media. Public education is asked to yield higher results with depleted resources. It is being asked to intervene in areas where it has little influence and control, such as housing and economic health, in the community it serves. And the outcry gets louder each election cycle. This has been done, at times, to promote the privatization of public education and to escalate political messages to move the approval dial with voters. Critical chatter about public education is heard on the sidelines at soccer games and on online forums. I believe it is time to re-evaluate this negative gamesmanship and chart our own course based on what is best for all people involved. Leaders will accomplish their greatest achievements through empowering people in pursuit of a noble mission, not by mere task completion: within a collaborative culture the collective pursuit of the well-being of everyone in the community. In *Flourish*, Martin Seligman writes well-being is about a positive disposition toward life that can be measured by the level of engagement we have in our own work, the richness and depth of our relationships with others, the meaning and purpose we find in our work and life, and finally, accomplishment—what can and have we achieved. Each dimension of well-being is embedded in a relationship with another person, place, or thing of importance to us.[12]

I believe we must make decisions for children's best interests first, but I also believe the second part of that equation is sometimes missed. We must prioritize the well-being of the teachers and staff. I believe we have swung from an adult-centric environment to a child-centric environment. While I think that is good, I also believe that we have swung so far that the important people who serve the clients, our children, have taken a backseat. One of the strengths of a relational leader is changing the cycle of downward spiraling discussions. A strong relational leader will, by their example, assist others through the positive pattern of their dialogue. Relational leaders, rather than constructing walls built of strife and hatred, are opening paths lined with understanding, beaming with confidence and showered with compassion.

Stating that you are a realist is just a nice way to say that you enjoy taking a negative stance. The positive leader does see the glass as half full and is the true realist. He or she is connecting with things that are strengths and a part of the organization. In appreciative organizing in public education, there is purpose in honoring past achievements. It allows people to observe, touch, see, feel, and remember the factors that are foundational and have helped create the success of the past. Continuously building relational capital by highlighting the strengths of an organization and its individuals follows and adds to a foundation for success.

## POSITIVE QUESTIONS

Voltaire wrote, "Judge a man by his questions rather than by his answers." The relational leader looks for ways to strengthen their organization by assisting others' growth through positive interactions that will encourage personal development. Positively stated questions open doors as well as minds. A positive question is an affirmatively stated question—a question that seeks to uncover and bring out the best in a person, a situation, or an organization. It is a question constructed around a topic that has been selected by a person or group—a topic that is fundamentally affirmative.[13] Relational leaders, like my former boss Max Ramos, regularly ask, "What are students doing well?" Other powerful questions that relational leaders ask are, "How are students using their strengths to succeed? Are they able to identify their own strengths?" Another simple question is "How might I help you?" Sounds innocent, but meaning it and being willing to take action, if necessary, makes all the difference. Questions can become one of your secret weapons for impacting the culture of your organization. Make them positive and well thought out. Never pass up the opportunity to ask a strength-based and/or life-reaffirming question.

Asking positive questions and using positive presuppositions (assuming competence) stimulates thought about what is possible and propels people to step into the amazing. Well thought out questions are more important than the answers they produce. Take the time to explore all the exercises at the end of book. Look at the steps of the "Asking Questions" exercise, and after practicing, add your own new questions in the exercises accompanying this chapter.

## DISPOSITIONS OF A RELATIONAL LEADER

Let's dig deeper into the dispositions of relational leadership. These dispositions are the key to creating a positive environment, which leads to personal and organizational growth. The dispositions that support developing relational capital are hopeful, caring, respectful, trustworthy, passionate, grateful, and kind. Doing what is right with people's best interest at the heart of your actions will generate relational capital and lead to success. Acknowledging, identifying, and using strengths to their fullest will create a positive environment.

## HOPEFUL

I am starting with hope because there is too little of it in many organizations. A relational leader who can provide hope has taken a significant step toward creating a brighter future. To be hopeful, we must have a vision of what success could look like in difficult times. Remember, it is easy to be hopeful when everything is going well. Your staff will need you to be your most hopeful self in the tough times. Relational leaders know that self-fulfilling prophecies are real. People must decide if they are fulfilling positive or negative visions of the future. Rumor has it that golf great Jack Nicklaus visualized each shot before he hit it. To see, hear, and feel a golf shot during and after you hit the ball is one thing, but to do those things in your mind's eye before the shot is another. Such vision can assist you on everything you set out to accomplish. Hope is often a poster on the school wall but it may often be a wish without a plan. When you are hopeful, you can visualize the success of a project or plan. C. Richard Snyder, a pioneer in positive psychology, shares that hope is developed through three elements working together. They are finding workable and understandable goals, finding a path to reach your goals, and believing that you can change and grow to meet your goals.[14]

Gamers create inventive and interesting worlds for avatars. It is time we create a more positive, beautiful, real place for our organizations and ourselves. Your goal should be to envision the success of the entire organization. It starts with being able to see concrete projects and situations. Your vision will contain an understanding of what it takes to accomplish the project. If you cannot visualize the outcome with some operational details, then you will just be wishing for something positive to happen. See in your mind's eye the parts of the project. See but also feel and hear what is going on when your project is successful.

Follow the steps in the "Visioning" exercise to practice and strengthen your skills. This will help you be even more successful when working on major projects or leading meetings and trainings. As you complete the exercises and take additional action on your own, you'll realize that you have already started to strengthen your relational capital through building hope. It is easy to see how doing some of the same exercises, with slight adjustments, can contribute to a positive home life as well. The more sure you are about where you are going, the easier it is to confidently speak to people around you.

## CARING AND KINDNESS

All caring people are not necessarily leaders, but relational leaders are always caring people. You must care deeply to succeed as you face the complexities of what it takes to be a relational leader. Have convictions for what you are doing as well as resoluteness about all the people with whom you connect. Being caring, kind, and empathetic is very important. The golden rule, treat others the way you would like others to treat you, might be a good way to start, but is not as powerful as the "platinum rule" developed by Tony Alessandra. The platinum rule is "Treat others the way they want to be treated." Ah-a! What a difference. The platinum rule accommodates the feelings of others. The focus of relationships shifts from "This is what I want, so I'll give everyone the same thing" to "Let me first understand what they want, and then I'll give it to them."[15] Know the people within your organization and care enough to put in the extra effort to communicate based on their interests and learning styles. This should help guide your actions. We are not thinking outside of ourselves by simply treating everyone the way we like to be treated. So the best service is not giving people what they ask for, but finding the best solution for them together.

Extra effort is always needed for a high-functioning relational leader. This simple quote speaks to us about the power of a smile and its importance in communicating who we are and why we are present. Author Denis Waitley states, "A smile is the light in your window that tells others that there is a caring, sharing person inside."[16] We must take advantage of our smile as the introduction to all things positive that are going to befall those whom we encounter. Show caring and kindness through your smile, of course, but also show your heart. Take the time to consider the importance of each of the steps in the "Smile Trial" exercise. It will help impact the climate of your workplace—and it's fun.

Establish a plan and create steps based on the "Four Steps of a Caring and Kind Leader" (below). The actions that you take are important whether you are at home or at work. Coming up with your own plan of ways to practice being a caring and kind leader will bring rewards.

| STEPS | ACTION |
|---|---|
| Lead with your heart | Show kindness and think about every situation and decide if you have the ability to round the harsh edges of situations for those around you. Practice an open body position. |
| Smile | William Arthur Ward stated, "A warm smile is the universal language of kindness." [17] Practice your smile until it is a part of your daily apparel. |
| Sympathize and Empathize | Always empathize when you have had the same kind of experiences, but it is good to have feelings for those who are experiencing things that might be unusual to you. Sometimes it is fortunate that we are unable to empathize with everything someone is going through. |
| Be attentive | We have talked about smiling and using an open body position, but we must let our caring nature guide all our actions as we work to be more attentive. This would include the way we walk and sit. The eye contact we give is a key to our with-it-ness during conversations. Listen carefully and attempt to instill in the speaker that they are the most important person to you at the time of your encounter. |

Chart 3.2  FOUR STEPS OF A CARING AND KIND LEADER

## GRATITUDE

I designed a gratitude workshop called "Leg-up People," which I have given to several thousand people over the past thirty years, and I am always amazed at the power of personal heroes. The workshop revolves around identifying people for whom you are extremely grateful and reaching out to them. A letter is nice, but the power of the exercise is built on a personal encounter. There have been countless reports of the person's recognized "personal hero" stating that the call made their year, month, week, or day. What could be better for our personal hero or for us? Donel Bisesi, my golf coach at Martinsville High School in Indiana, was one of those people in my life. I was working with my wife to clean out the garage and ran across some memorabilia from my childhood. We found some junior high and high school clippings, pictures, yearbooks, and report cards that my father had kept over the years. I work hard at being an upbeat and positive person, but after breathing the dust and going back down memory lane, I was feeling more than a little melancholy when we sat down to dinner. I told my wife that junior high was not a very positive time for me at school or at home. I sat there and thought about what made the difference between my junior high and high school experiences, because my home situation for several of those years remained the same. I realized that it was not one of my academic teachers but my golf coach who made the difference.

I was an inexperienced freshman in whom the coach saw potential. I had thanked Coach Bisesi before, but this time I wrote him a letter and told him that he had created purpose and instilled in me that I was, and could be, special. Coach Bisesi was my personal hero who through his time and dedication changed the next four years of my life. The letter traveled from Florida to Indiana and back to Florida where Coach Bisesi was wintering and going through radiation treatment. He said he read the letter over and over again. He gave me a call on the very day he received the well-traveled letter. When we reach out to express gratitude we never know how important it will be in someone's life. Find and thank the Donel Bisesis in your life.

Cicero wrote, "Gratitude is not only the greatest of virtues, but the parent of all others." On most days, we must choose to look at the positive aspects of the day or our life. We become focused on our own organization, department, or school. An important question might be, how are we helping the students, teachers, or administrators at neighboring schools or districts? We not only create an example of selflessness, but by reaching out to others, also demonstrate an attitude of helpfulness, thus creating a climate of gratitude. Being grateful is one thing but taking action to help others is quite another.

Nelson Henderson restates an old Greek proverb very well: "The true meaning of life is to plant trees under whose shade you do not expect to sit." Educators often find themselves, because of the immense importance of their work on behalf of students, having several long-term goals from which they might never harvest the fruits. This makes leading, motivating, and providing vision for those types of efforts even more important. Ralph Waldo Emerson wrote: "Cultivate the habit of being grateful for every good thing that comes to you, and to give thanks continuously. And because all things have contributed to your advancement, you should include all things in your gratitude." Take time and practice being grateful each day through the powerful "Gratitude" exercise and follow-up "Saying Thank You" exercise. "It is not happy people that are thankful. It is thankful people that are happy."

## TRUST AND RESPECT

I learned the power of respect in business from William "Bill" Kipple, a golf professional in Terre Haute and Brazil, Indiana. I learned that someone who had made a mistake could be a thankful and genuinely respectful person to everyone he encountered. While working for him during college at Forest Park Golf Course in Brazil, Indiana, I had to go into the clubhouse to tell him that I had just wrecked the brand-new tractor that was on loan to the golf course. The bad part was that my friend Mike Morgan and I had been racing the tractors as we were taking them back to the shed. The manner in which Bill handled the situation will stick with me for the rest of my life. While I wanted to accept the consequences of my action, he insisted that it was his responsibility to oversee the appropriate use of borrowed equipment. His action not only demonstrated forgiveness for me, he showed me that sometimes a leader might have to take responsibility for the actions of others, since the leader is ultimately responsible even though the leader is not in control 100 percent of the time. I have never forgotten the importance of the respect he demonstrated as a relational leader to me.

The relational leader develops trust, which leads to deeper respect when people know that their leader's heart is good. Honesty is the foundation on which trust is built, and true respect will only come to leaders who are consistently kind, honest, and trusting themselves. Relational leaders know that their titles do not give them the influence they seek. The relational leader understands that respect is established over time and numerous encounters and can be undone in an instant. How well you work with others is paramount to your success as well as the success of the organization. The relational leader understands that his example can be his downfall or one of his most influential assets. Never miss a chance to do an unpopular job or a job that some might think is below their station. There are no jobs in an organization that are beneath anyone. We all know the need for amazing teachers and administrators, but for an organization to be successful, every job, including that of custodian, bus driver, and food service worker, must not be overlooked for their contribution to the overall environment and its success. When the principal is willing to stand out in the rain at car duty when it is not their normal assignment, people take notice. George Herbert leaves us with the reminder that "good words are worth much and cost little." Unselfish actions and positive words show respect and develop high levels of trust.

Our words can promote trust. Albert Einstein wisely said, "I speak to everyone in the same way, whether he is the garbage man or the president of the university." Why would any one person deserve less kindness, honesty, and respect than another? You never know whom you are impacting on a day-to-day basis. Think about not only how our words promote trust, but our thoughts as well. Before a conference or encounter, think about what would occur if the person with whom you are conferencing could hear your thoughts. The exercise "Everyone Can Hear My Thoughts" is difficult and powerful.

Your relational capital is on the rise when you combine gratitude and respect with a caring nature while developing hope in others. You will take into account that this is a journey and each step forward will help everyone you come into contact with.

## HOPE AND PASSION

Hope is not the least of the dispositions but incorporates all of the others to accomplish its mission. I looked at the research, studied plans and goals, reviewed my core beliefs, remembered past success, and then said a prayer that I would be the encourager the staff needed. I have stood in front of a mirror and in front of other people in my inner group practicing and convincing them that our efforts would produce positive results. One time I even dressed up in a cape and wild hat and had a guitar as I kicked off the Hope Tour for the upcoming year. On the back of the concert T-shirts were the strategies we would use to help us reach even greater success. My passion, hard work, and willingness to be just a little crazy helped us take the next steps to our success. My staff believed that a crazy principal who was dancing and playing air guitar would be with them each and every step of the way, providing the training, support, and resources necessary for success. They had hope, and combined with hard work focused on specific goals, it translated into success.

## KEY SUPPORTIVE QUALITIES

Relational leaders know that being purposeful, goal oriented, tenacious, and resilient provides the key support needed for relational capital to flourish.

The four supportive qualities are noted here.

| 4 Key Supportive Qualities |
| :---: |
| Purposeful |
| Goal Oriented |
| Tenacious |
| Resilient |

## PURPOSEFUL AND GOAL ORIENTED

For twelve years, I had the privilege of working with an amazing person, Kara Smucker, who epitomized each of these key supportive qualities. While I was the principal, she held the positions of intermediate teacher, reading specialist, writing specialist, curriculum specialist, and assistant principal at Seven Springs Elementary and Chasco Elementary Schools in Pasco County, Florida. She influenced the work on every major curriculum project in our high-needs school. She knew that we must not only care about where we were going but must care deeply about whom we are going there with. She understood that we must care about who we are leading if we expect anyone to follow for very long. She had a laser focus to complement her dedication to powerful positive relationships. Success can be achieved in any model when you are focused on a goal with a clear understanding of how to get there and a willingness to do the necessary work with people you care about.

School leaders have a laser focus on their goal of raising

student achievement and school improvement. They need the same laser-focused effort on developing relationships. In her second term as principal, Smucker was transferred to a high-needs school with the goal of arresting the negative achievement slide of the school. She realized that she had to take action quickly, but the first step was getting to know the staff and developing new relationships.

Most of us would agree that people matter most, and anything can be done with the correct motivation and right goals. I appeal to you that the goal focus must be for the right reasons, that people matter most, and to do anything that can be sustained, you must have the correct motivation. It must be done because it is the right thing to do, not because it is expedient or might help you politically. It must be noted that even though you will get improved results in your school or organization by building your relational skills, it still must be done because it is the right thing to do, not the thing to do to get good results.

Having a strong goal focus means understanding the importance of measurable results. Be willing to try new things that develop people for the sake of their well-being while pursuing those goal-focused results. When you create an organization where it is understood that true inquiry is not only allowed but encouraged, new goals emerge and evolve. The beauty of an organization built on that type of freedom and support is the amazing benefits that end up happening that you never planned.

An experienced assistant principal in an elementary school that had received an F the year before was working on a major project to raise math scores. At the end of September, six third-grade teachers came to him and said they were all considering quitting because the job was so difficult and they did not think they could succeed. He took the news very hard and told them it was time to reassess their goals and situation. It was a risky venture, but he had an appreciative inquiry mini-summit with the team and started fresh with the group. The combination of being heard and framing their actions on the strengths and dreams of the team led to many new strategies and approaches on the original project, and ultimately student achievement in math rose. The teachers started working on an authentic problem-based learning approach in which they took a much more facilitative role. They held intensive groups for some students and taught short lessons as needed to assist the students who were now tracking their own personal growth and working as a team to complete important projects. Excitement grew, and the fourth-grade team asked for help so that they could start to work in the same way. Some large gains were being realized on students' formative assessments, and students were excited to be with the teachers in their classes. Additionally, all six teachers asked to come back, work together, and loop with the same students to the next grade.

People's potential is released by trust and openness, not restriction and bureaucracy. Fear prohibits many from trying and inhibits some leaders from allowing anything that is not written in a book. Solid library research is a good place to start, but creating what goes into the book is even more important. Relational leaders create safe environments where failure is accepted as a part of learning. Malcolm Gladwell writes, "We prematurely write off people as failures. We are too much in awe of those who succeed and far too dismissive of those who fail." Failing the right way is failing with excellent intentions, based on good research, accompanied by hard work while including others. Goals set on these foundational blocks might feel like a failure to the initiator, but they are merely not as successful as the initiator might have hoped or imagined; not a total failure in any sense.

Goals and nonnegotiable parameters go together under expectations that impact an organization. Have as few non-negotiable dictums as possible and communicate them in an open way. For example, you might have an expectation that there is an organizational commitment to professional growth and development. One thing the relational leader must do is to participate fully in training himself or herself, whether as a participant or presenter. They must have positive discussions about professional development opportunities. After communicating the expectation of professional growth, the more difficult question must be asked: How do individual people want to learn and how do they learn best? Attention to personalizing training for educators is difficult but will secure the best results.

Regardless of individual styles, the goals must be clear and well communicated. Goal-oriented leaders are action oriented. Having a well-written goal and communicating it in several ways does very little without a commitment to action. Goal orientation and action orientation go hand in hand and are incredibly important for a relational leader's success.

## TENACIOUS AND RESILIENT

Merriam-Webster defines the quality of being *tenacious* as being someone or something that is "not easily pulled apart," someone who will "continue for a long time" and is "very determined to do something." It is someone who is "seeking something valued or desired." The two dispositions, tenacity and resilience, hold some things in common, but the difference is tenacious people stick to the course and resilient people have an ability to bounce back from adversity. For relational leadership, I like the combination of determination while seeking something valued. Stick-to-it-ness, grit, dogged determination, perseverance, and the ability to bounce back from adverse situations are amazing human qualities to aspire to. Research psychologist and MacArthur fellow Angela Duckworth's research on grit is extremely beneficial in this area. The twelve-item grit survey is a free tool that can give you insight.

There are times when all levels of school leadership can push staff to be more random and scattered because of the multitude of different activities. Every school administrator knows there are days when they could go to their office with no plans or goals and work extremely hard just reacting to all the situations that come up during the day. We have to strive to find some quiet time and work on big goals or projects that cannot just be checked off a list at the end of the day. There must be a time when we stick with our project and keep to the course of action we have set for our work. This does not mean we can revert to being stubborn and unwilling to analyze if something is working well or not. "It's not clear what makes some people grittier than others, but Angela Duckworth believes grit is something people can probably learn."[18]

> Your mindset is critical to increasing your tenacity and resilience. A "fixed mindset" assumes that our character, intelligence, and creative ability are static givens that we can't change in any meaningful way . . . A "growth mindset," on the other hand, thrives on challenge and sees failure not as evidence of unintelligence but as a heartening springboard for growth and for stretching our existing abilities. Out of these two mindsets, which we manifest from a very early age, springs a great deal of our behavior, our relationship with success and failure in both professional and personal contexts, and ultimately our capacity for happiness.[19]

Relational leaders tend to be much more growth oriented in nature and believe they can increase their skills. Because of this, they know that with tenacious effort they can become highly successful leaders in an appreciative organization.

## DO IT AGAIN, AND AGAIN, AND AGAIN

Practicing the exercises provided at the end of the book is a necessity for your development as a relational leader. In his best-selling book *Outliers*, Malcolm Gladwell talks about the importance of putting in ten thousand hours of practice to become an expert. Relational leaders have an advantage in that they can gain their ten thousand hours of practice at work as well as at home. The table below will give us some idea of how quickly we can accumulate the number of hours necessary to become experts. To become a great relational leader, you must practice your craft. Gladwell writes, "Practice isn't the thing you do once you're good. It's the thing you do that makes you good." Leadership exercises are just like other types of exercises; they are good for you, but you have to do them. It is critical as we think about our own personal plan of action—whether we step up, lean in, or jump in. If we step up to the edge and observe, we then must really think about and plan what we will do. If we lean in, we then try some of the exercises and activities and consider making a bigger commitment. If you decide to jump in. then do just that—jump in completely. Start to live the activities and exercises. Immerse yourself in the literature and start on the path to gain ten thousand hours of practice to become an expert. Like any type of exercise, we must burn some calories, only this time we are burning relational calories. Now it is time to practice and create positive habits of which we will be proud and which will also help us as leaders and as people. Only tenacious relational leaders can get to their ten thousand hours of practice. See how you can reach expertise in less than four years of practice.

| Goal for Total Amount of Practice Needed to Reach Expertise | Number of Hours of Practice per Day | Number of Days | Number of Weeks | Number of Years |
|---|---|---|---|---|
| 10,000 hours | 4 hours | 2,500 days (if you only practice during the week) | 500 weeks | less than 10 years |
| 10,000 hours | 8 hours | 1,250 days (if you only practice during the week) | 250 weeks | less than 5 years |

Chart 3.3  PRACTICE AND MORE PRACTICE

## BENEFITS OF RELATIONAL LEADING: JOY AND WELL-BEING

As we consider our separate paths to becoming a more enlightened relational leader, we recognize that there is something much more meaningful at stake than just incorporating the dispositions and key supportive qualities. I want you to be fulfilled and joyful and to have fun at work and home. I want you to be successful day to day and year to year.

In the short story "De Daumier-Smith's Blue Period," J. D. Salinger wrote, "The fact is always obvious much too late, but the most singular difference between happiness and joy is that happiness is a solid and joy a liquid." I find that to be an interesting description. Merriam-Webster defines *joy* as "the emotion evoked by well-being, success, or good fortune or by the prospect of possessing what one desires" and "a feeling of great happiness." I want you to lead like you know that you are destined to have good fortune and success. Day to day and year to year, you are leading from a place of well-being, success, and good fortune. If you are leading for the mere purpose of raising test scores, you may be happy one year. However, if you lead school improvement efforts long enough, you will surely be sad or depressed at some time in your career. The only way to avoid this is to get great test scores your first year as a principal and then retire.

A relational leader has their focus on achievement but an equal and more enlightened focus on doing and being a positive person who keeps individuals at the forefront of their goals and beliefs. If you lead with a focus on serving others, following a moral imperative of equity and excellence for all students while striving to be a relational leader, then good things will ensue each and every year. It is the only way to find joy in a constantly changing system where the rules are being shifted year after year with little concern for the dedicated practitioners and the students they serve. Your joy comes from who you are becoming and how you treat the people you have the privilege to work with.

No state agency or school district can dictate who you are or predict your legacy. The "Legacy" exercise is for everyone no matter what stage of career this books finds you. Spread joy through your smile and demeanor without the expectation of anything in return. Everyone deserves your very best. Your very best includes leading with joy. To give anything less is disrespectful to the amazing gift each of us has been given and the joy we deserve.

The impact of our personal growth and development affects the entire organization. School leaders must understand that being an example of positive actions and sharing stories of hope based upon strengths is pivotal in creating an environment of success. Dean Koontz, a *New York Times* best-selling author, uses the following fictional epigraph in *From the Corner of His Eye*:

> Each smallest act of kindness reverberates across great distances and spans of time, affecting lives unknown to the one whose generous spirit was the source of this good echo, because kindness is passed on and grows each time it's passed, until a simple courtesy becomes an act of selfless courage years later and far away.

And so we influence, and so we grow.

### PRACTICE BEING

Take an opportunity to work through the exercises and activities, and most of all, practice being. Relational leadership networks have unlimited potential because of the power of positive interaction multiplied through many people. Building a positive and caring culture because people respect you is not luck. It is essential to have a relational leader if we expect to have an appreciative organization. Relational leaders are convinced that they can influence in a very positive way the DNA of their organization. I believe that relational leadership is the alchemy of positive change and at the core of the appreciative organization. Lead on!

# CHAPTER FOUR
## The Fourth Sphere of AO
### Generative Learning and Capacity Building
Leonard C. Burrello

## ENDING THE BLAME GAME

It's easy to blame the schools. Public education is the faceless culprit invoked at PTA meetings and in stump speeches in Iowa. Drop-out rates increasing, blame the schools. Scandinavian students outranking us in math and science, blame the schools. Graduates not prepared for twenty-first-century jobs, blame the schools. College freshmen require remedial courses, you guessed it. This is a game with no winners, but everyone wants to play. Everyone is an expert because everyone has been to school.

The "prize" is a constant drumbeat of criticism that feeds a downward spiral in vulnerable communities in need of hope and better outcomes. Educators' morale has been lowered and competence has been questioned from school board meetings to the halls of state legislatures and Congress. They call for more accountability, more student testing tied to teacher performance and charter schools that have less accountability and regulations. They think this will show public schools the way to success. Policy leaders are too cynical about the possibilities and the opportunities for improvement. Educational leadership needs more Robert Kennedy and less Eeyore to turn around communities caught in generational poverty and neglect. We have a choice. We can continue to blame schools for contributing to this cycle or build upon their strengths to create beacons for success.

Appreciative Organizing, as a generative process, taps into

educators' desire to make a difference in the lives of children and youth. Generative learning is the means relational leaders use to inspire and encourage the co-construction of new knowledge, skills, and processes to accelerate student learning. Generativity is Appreciative Inquiry at its best.

The relational leader finds generative affirming topics that are stimulating, meaningful, and energizing and can engage educators and school stakeholders. The relational leader utilizes generative questions, not questions that affix blame or hold educators accountable for conditions or previous reform initiatives out of their control. Questions that lead to generative conversations result in actions supported by all stakeholders. Reconnecting the school to the community is what Anthony Bryk argues for in his studies of the Chicago reform movement. This reconnection must come early in any reform. Leaders must be inclusive of all stakeholders, promote free expression, and invent new ways of organizing the committed to the work. They need to continue to invite the more skeptical community members to participate. This continuous process of engagement leads to stakeholder ownership and commitment. But this will only occur through genuine and authentic collaborative teaming of insiders and outsiders. The leadership's commitment will be tested often in the early stages of reengagement before stemming the critical spiral that results from the blame game.[1]

## TENETS OF GENERATIVITY

The tenets of generative learning began in the seventies. I won't go back to the Vietnam era, but I want to frame the generative learning sphere with a set of assumptions suggested by Kenneth Gergen, the director of the Taos Institute, which has published many books on Appreciative Inquiry scholarship. Gergen defines generative theory as "the capacity to challenge the guiding assumptions of the culture, to raise fundamental questions regarding contemporary social life, to foster re-consideration of that which is 'taken for granted' and thereby furnish new alternatives for social actions."[2]

Former MIT professor Donald Schön described generativity as "nothing less than how we come to see things in new ways." Schön argues "how problems are addressed is powerfully influenced by the metaphors and frames used to describe them. From all this, it follows that problem setting matters." The ways in which "we set social problems determine both the kinds of purposes and values we seek to realize, and the directions in which we seek solutions." Contrary to the problem-solving perspective, "problems are not given, nor are they reducible to arbitrary choices that lie beyond inquiry. We set problems through the stories we tell—stories whose problem-setting potency derives at least in some cases from generative metaphors."[3]

In early writing AI was described by Frank Barrett and David Cooperrider as a form of inquiry that would "acknowledge the impact of generative metaphor."[4] Rather than trying to explain the past, AI offers a method for the generative creation of new ideas, perceptions, metaphors, images, and theories that furnished better alternatives for organizational actions.[5] Peter Senge, whose book *The Fifth Discipline* became popular with corporate managers in the early 1990s, joined the stream of thinkers arguing that generative learning rather than adaptive learning is needed more today given the unprecedented change we are experiencing.[6] Change is characterized by volatility, uncertainty, complexity, and ambiguity. Today we use the acronym VUCA. The idea has roots in the armed services. I first read about VUCA in the work of technologist Denise Caron.[7] VUCA affects most if not all organizations, including schools. Since 2002, schools have continued to be heavily regulated, which hinders innovative thinking and action. School leaders have become extremely good adaptive learners. They have made adaptive responses to external demands for accountability during the severe fiscal constraints of the Great Recession of the last seven years. These changes have been largely incremental and oriented toward maintaining the status quo.

## TENETS IN ACTION

Recently our writing team has been conducting interviews with outstanding superintendents and administrators from California, Florida, Mississippi, Indiana, Illinois, Tennessee, Texas, and Colorado to enrich our understanding of appreciative organizing in public schools. These leaders share their successes in an era of VUCA. We have discovered the positive core and strengths of these districts and their schools. They all engage generative inquiry, but they see the future differently. Bill Jensen, the secondary director of education in Columbus, Indiana, simply stated, "We believe in student variability." This district belief helped staff decide on an instructional framework known as Universal Design for Learning (UDL). UDL embraces student differences and helps teachers design instruction that takes into account how different students access and represent what and how they learn, and how and why they stay engaged in their own learning. Jensen concludes, "we believe students should be architects of their own learning. That is our focus and our strength."[8]

In another project, I have been working with graduate students visiting "turnaround schools" in the ten districts that make up the Central Florida School Boards Coalition. Relational leadership was evident as we watched principals interact with school staff and community: from construction workers to visitors from local businesses to human resources to, of course, their faculty. The principals advocated high levels of teacher and student engagement and revised their practices and responses to lift historically low levels of student achievement and poor behavioral choices. Furthermore they raised the level of teacher expectations, supported data-based instructional decision making, and reconnected families who had lost their connection to the public schools. Plano, Texas, superintendent Brian Binggeli calls this "leading from the middle." Binggeli sharpened his AO leadership skill while superintendent of Brevard County, Florida. In Brevard he asked his staff, both professional and classified, principals, and other school leaders to come together and find new ways of being more effective, responsive, and efficient. His examples went from collaborative planning across grade levels in elementary and middle schools, to departments of disciplinary or content-focused teams, to construction workers, bus drivers, and custodians. What they all had in common was a commitment to finding a better way of working together—coconstructing plans and interventions and soliciting feedback to track their progress.[9] One of Binggeli's principals, Michael Miller, has been on the job some sixteen years now. He inherited a school whose staff had little confidence and low morale and whose students performed poorly. In sixteen years on the job he has released only one teacher, and that was in the first year. Using a positive, strength-based approach, from the first year forward he has built a staff that is confident, engaged, and high performing. The only demand he made of staff was clear, instructional decision making based upon weekly formative assessment calibrated to individual student proficiencies. Miller noted that data is the lifeblood of their work; it informs instruction daily. Superintendent Binngeli called Miller the "King of Data." His school outperformed many other top schools in Brevard county, the forty-seventh largest district in the country.

Both leaders agree that school culture is key. "It starts with a belief that people need to be empowered to do what they think is right," Binggeli says, "because it's all about cultural change, and it comes with changing work processes and ongoing evaluation of them."[10]

The new incoming superintendent of Burbank, California, Matt Hill, when asked about the positive core of his former district, Los Angeles Unified, agreed that a tight culture with clear values was apparent to him. He felt the way forward in LAUSD was to capitalize on the longevity of staff who are shining stars and invite them to share their success by promoting innovative practices they have developed district-wide.[11]

I took Binggeli's advice about "leading from the middle" to my work in Meridian, Mississippi, with Superintendent Dr. Alvin Taylor.[12] Taylor's initial goal was to bring stability to a district that had had five superintendents in seven years. In year three, he wanted to bring Meridian's decentralized and relatively independent thirteen schools together into an integrated, single system. Historically Meridian schools had operated under a survival of the fittest mentality, competing for finite resources. Taylor hosted a summer event for fifty-two district and school leaders who formed five work groups to study and learn together how to implement the district's newly established Compass Framework. His top district administrators (personnel, curriculum, operations, school-based administrators, and teacher leaders) were placed into heterogeneous working groups of professional and classified staff to produce prototypes that would guide collaborative improvement. Whatever came out of a work group needed to pass whole group muster and pilot testing before implementation was set in motion. The administrators crafted responses to reading and math blocks, inclusive education, and community engagement. Testing them out together has increased ownership and acceptance in a climate of collaboration, leading to ownership of the Compass Framework.

In a secondary school district in Illinois, Superintendent Michael Riggle recalled how a powder puff football team's hazing incident that occurred off-site spilled into the district the next week. It became the basis of a generative inquiry into how all district curricular and extracurricular activities were impacting students. Using his appreciative capacity, he took a single negative example of student behavior, bullying, and reframed it as a question of student well-being. Riggle's goal was to increase student aspirations for more positive and fulfilling experiences across all activities. He found that freshmen band students were just as frightened to attend summer band camp off campus as were junior girls to participate in powder puff football games.[13]

In the *Appreciative Inquiry Handbook: For Leaders of Change*, David Cooperrider, Diana Whitney, and Jacqueline Stavros write that organizations move toward what they study and that AI focuses on the best of the organization, its positive core. Generative learning determines how a school or district chooses what it is going to study or inquire about. Leaders in Florida and Mississippi have zeroed in on affirmative topics that recognize what they have done well, which helps to determine what they want to do next.[14]

Cooperrider, Whitney, and Stavros believe that the positive core of organizational life is a key resource that has gone unrecognized in organizational development or change management.[15] "AI has demonstrated that human systems grow in the direction of their persistent inquiries, and this propensity is strongest and most sustainable when the means and ends of inquiry are positively correlated."[16] In chapter two, Linda Beitz wrote that the concept of the positive core cuts through all phases of the 4-D cycle:

Discovery—What gives life?
Dream—What might be, or what can we imagine?
Design—How can it be?
Destiny—How to empower, learn, and adjust or improvise?

I've brainstormed a list of attributes of a positive core school or district:

- Having a clear purpose and core values that are publically held such as a commitment to socially and ethically responsible citizenship

- Students winning recognition for their achievements in statewide competitions

- Getting students into the right college for success

- Being innovative in personalizing learning for all students and teaching social justice for all

- Distributing leadership across professional and classified staff

- Successfully moving students in tier two supplemental instruction

- Hiring and retaining new teachers with an innovative salary schedule

- Having collaborative professional learning communities where teachers learn and share their practice publicly

- Parents expressing their satisfaction with the quality of the education

- Establishing partnerships with external stakeholders, institutions of higher education, and other districts

- Being fiscally responsible to the community

- Having well-maintained facilities

- Being a fully inclusive school district where all means all!

## GENERATIVE PROCESSES

The first step for an AO process work team is selecting the affirmative topic and describing the future state that you want to bring into being. The team's choice of affirmative topic should build upon past success. An example of a school accomplishment might be placing students in prestigious colleges and universities. The purpose of this process is to discover the positive core of the system while celebrating and building on success and creating energy for inquiry into the future. The positive core in schools is largely tied to its people and their innovations in teaching and learning. Yet, the systems they build are an essential part of the positive core as well. Examples might be a formative assessment process, a senior project protocol, or the continuous improvement platform. While we prefer to see the whole community of stakeholders choosing the study topics, for many reasons—urgency, external pressures, lack of trust—a small group of leaders might select the topic. For example, the Meridian top leaders, guided by the board's goals, selected the affirmative topics. Or in the Williston, Vermont, example discussed in chapter one, the local school board and a teacher team selected the affirmative topics. In each process, the designated leaders had to work through all relevant stakeholder groups to get their buy-in. Stakeholder commitment was necessary to advance the conversation and ultimately the new work that emerged.

Once the affirmative topic and the positive core are identified, then the conversations can move to describing the future in concrete terms. Develop images that make the dream a reality. (Social psychologists suggest imagining a desired future state and what life would be like—working, learning, living in it.) This imaginative role-playing is popular in the training of athletes. The tight end and wide receivers must catch the football by imagining it directly into their hands. Or as John Mann has written about, Jack Nicklaus imagining the golf shot. And then they ask teams to connect that future state with what is happening now. They ask, "What actions have already been taken? What resources do we have? What do we need? What do we know? What don't we know?"

Who does the imagining is important. It cannot be restricted to a small group at the top; all levels of stakeholders need to be engaged in imagining and committing. Meridian superintendent Alvin Taylor's district leadership team established the original five topics, but after two days of thinking and working together the enlarged team of more than fifty-two district and school leaders created a more energized set of affirmative topics. Those revised topics form the body of their work today. Teachers at every school were given a full day to engage these same topics in light of the district purpose and core values. Each school was asked to build them into their school improvement plans. District forums invited parents and the community from each school to hear what these purpose and core values meant for them and their children. All of these forums use the tenets of generative learning to increase the number of diverse perspectives heard and debated. The goal is to gain a commitment to their implementation and application.

Here are the original topics the Meridian district team brainstormed contrasted with the revisions by the complete district team following a generative process of engagement.[17]

| ORIGINAL TOPICS | TEAM TOPICS |
| --- | --- |
| Increase reading scores | Relentlessly pursue literacy |
| Become one district | Become an exceptional district |
| Increase communication between school and district leadership | Create a culture of trust and respect that balances centralization with school autonomy |
| Hire and retain teaching staff to lower turnover rates | Build partnerships with universities to better prepare teachers for urban schools |
| Create district level guidance on instruction in math and reading supported by district instructional specialists | Build grade level / departmental teams that rely on teacher leaders in each school to lead collaborative planning supported by district-level specialist as needed |

Cooperrider, Whitney, and Stavros offer three sets of criteria for teams to consider in any organizational development work. We list them with permission of the authors.[18]

### Main Points

- Topic choice is a fateful act
- Organizations move in the direction of inquiry
- Vocabulary is not just semantics; words create worlds
- People commit to topics they helped develop
- Everyone is an active participant
- Diversity is essential

### Critical Choice

- Build a representative steering committee or start with senior executive–level team or involve the whole system where possible
- While is it difficult to involve everyone, inviting community members to participate is an essentially strategy of engagement that increases awareness and hopefully some level of support at the ballot box for funding increases to support schools.

### Rules of Thumb

- No more than five topics are finally selected
- Topics are phrased in affirmative terms
- Topic is driven by curiosity—spirit of discovery
- Topic is genuinely desired. People want to see it grow

- Topic is consistent with the overall organizational direction and its intentions
- Topic choice involves those that have an important stake in the future
- Topic choice should take up to two days

Meridian leadership decided to "lead from the middle" by asking its fifty-two-district professional and classified staff to build a district framework to bring all parts of the total system together under one umbrella. With one set of core values and beliefs, one set of nonnegotiable practices, and one set of work goals for the year, they put in motion a district improvement plan to unify thirteen schools into a single whole system. This new system is grounded in a culture of trust and respect rather than fear and retribution. All of the main points listed above were considered in that decision.

Once the framework was developed, the district leadership team deliberately set out to engage all staff, professional and classified, from secretaries to custodians and bus drivers. They were able to commit to a set of five topics that eventually were embraced by 87 percent of the teaching staff. The classified staff assessment is recommended after one year.

In regard to the rules of thumb, they selected five topics, phrased in affirmative terms, and revisions were made and reaffirmed by the total group then disseminated for whole-system implementation. As the rules of thumb suggest, keeping the work real and alive and engaging takes constant vigilance requiring regular reinforcement. As Superintendent Binggeli suggested, "we must remind staff of the nobleness of their mission."[19]

## APPRECIATIVE COMPETENCIES AND
## GENERATIVE LEARNING

Frank Barrett defined *appreciation* as "the art of discovering and valuing those factors that give life to the organization, of identifying what is best in the current organization."[20] Creating an appreciative culture is contagious; it creates what Peter Senge calls "generative conversations," as inquiries expand from valuing the best of "what is" to envisioning "what might be."[21] While problem solving emphasizes a dispassionate and objective separation between observers and the observed, appreciation is a passionate, absorbing endeavor. Appreciation inquiry involves investing emotional and cognitive energy to create a positive image of a desired future.

Barrett describes his theory of competency in an appreciative world. This includes four types: affirmative, expansive, generative, and collaborative.[22] Affirmative competency enables a strength-based approach grounded in the positive, building on what we are already doing. Uncovering the good in a bad school or district is difficult for sure, but the starting point has to be with the resources that you already have. School reform models have included the concept of a critical mass of the talented and committed that are needed to build a foundation for success.

Expansive competency enables you to extend your resources from what they do to applying them to what you still want to accomplish. A total rebuilding might be necessary in a few failing schools and districts, but the key is to find the way to build from what you have.

Generative competency enables you to build using the positive core of the organization. It often leads to discoveries a single small group might not make on their own. If significant and meaningful development is the goal, generative learning brings multiple perspectives and sets of expertise to bear on the unforeseen, the unknowable. It generates the energy to move the most difficult schools to engage in the hard work of transformative change.

Collaborative competency leads to an open invitation to all stakeholders to bring their expertise to the change movement. The speed of change is rooted in the amount of trust and respect that lies in the culture. School districts in Warren Township and Columbus, Indiana, and Meridian, Mississippi, offer examples of each competency.

## AFFIRMATIVE AND EXPANSIVE COMPETENCIES

Warren Township, located on the outskirts of Indianapolis, is an example of both affirmative and expansive competencies because their affirmative topic grew out of the district's well-established positive core, its own full-scale eight-step instructional model. With this model Superintendent Dena Cushenberry built upon the integrated multitier system of support to get all students over the proficiency bar. For example, in 2012–2013, 96 percent of third graders (excluding exempt students) passed the state proficiency examination. One hundred students needed tutoring the following summer to meet their proficiency goal, and thirty-three needed an additional year of support in fourth grade with a reading interventionist. Only one student in this cohort of more than eight hundred students was retained in fourth grade.

This district also shows expansive competency as it extends its instructional model into a twenty-first-century integrated, blended digital learning platform. Using a highly competitive federal grant, the superintendent and her staff are infusing technology and digital content into the classrooms. The goal is threefold: first, to increase the degree of student-centered planning; second, to increase rapid data retrieval; and third, to add technology support so students meet the new College and Career Readiness Standards (CCRS) at their grade or content area. While some states and many districts have waited for their governors and legislatures to adopt or opt out of the CCRS and the accompanying assessment consortium, Warren Township has been going full steam since 2010.

I discovered another example of affirmative and expansive competencies in Columbus, Indiana. This district leadership team used the Great Recession and the pressure to be more accountable for all student learning to pilot test an instructional framework known as Universal Design for Learning (UDL). In the early 2008, they extended their UDL pilot test to include more schools, and when they saw that students with disabilities improved their proficiency rates by 100 percent, they took the model to scale across the entire district. Their model is renowned. Columbus schools receive educators from around the world to observe how their personalized learning system succeeds within a high-stakes testing world. They used the federal and state policy as an impetus to not only respond to increasing accountability demands but to create an instructional model that led to whole system coherence and instructional stability.

## GENERATIVE COMPETENCE AND COLLABORATIVE COMPETENCE AO

Organizations with generative competence construct integrative systems that allow members to see the consequences of their actions, to recognize that they are making a meaningful contribution, and to experience a sense of progress. Organizations with collaborative competence create forums in which members exchange diverse perspectives in ongoing dialogue.

Bartholomew County Community Schools in Columbus, Indiana, is an example of generative competence as well. The school district's vision and core values speak to students as architects of their own learning. To do this they needed to adopt an integrated system of instruction that thrives on variability and gives guidance to teachers and students allowing them to see the consequences of their actions, to recognize that they are making a meaningful contribution, and to experience a sense of progress. A component of the integrated system is the teacher evaluation system that the district designed. Their breakdown:

- 50 percent quality of teacher implementation of UDL
- 25 percent student performance on standardized tests
- 25 percent teacher contributions to their professional learning community

Their annual professional development workshop is another component of their integrated system. It supports new teacher induction, re-teaching, and enrichment for current practitioners of UDL.

The Meridian, Mississippi, school district offers us the example of a collaborative competence where none existed before. The instability of leadership at the district level, lawsuits, and decentralization of curriculum and instruction without any system guidance led to principals acting as individual entrepreneurs. Superintendent Taylor's first goal was to build a culture of trust and respect. District Compass framework work groups used a positive strength-based approach within an AO mind-set to align school and district work in hopes of changing the culture of district to school relations.[23]

The emerging proposals of these district teams became generative. In addition to a work group on the district-school culture and community engagement, other goals include developing the integrative systems linking instructional time with quality instruction and classroom walkthroughs. My colleague, Karmen Mills and I worked with the district team to reinforce the meaning of this new work and to track its progress. After one year of meetings, each work group had improvement solutions from math literacy to community engagement. The other work groups on inclusive school practices and on improving reading performance are continuing next year with some modification. Work groups engaged a weighty list of affirmative topics across all schools—where many of these professionals had never collaborated before. While still in its infancy, the work in Meridian shows great promise. Each school principal led their staff orientation to the district's new purpose and core values and participated in bringing community members into the Compass framework.

The pressure on local leaders is great. Can these dedicated professionals use AO principles to move from a D+/C- district to a B district in the next two years? Everyone is awaiting the final results, but progress is evident, and the path is now clear. For the first time in many years collaborative competency is growing and making a difference in Meridian.

It is my belief that sustainability is about finding the positive core and public schools using formative assessment data. Armed with data, we climb an implementation ladder where each rung raises the stakes from pilots to initial testing to whole system implementation. Not only is student performance data crucial, so is team development and student, teacher, and parent engagement and satisfaction. Ultimately we need to provide evidence related to all of our goals, not just student performance.

John Mann and I created a school-level rather than a district-level affirmative competence exercise to practice. Find it at the end of the book.

## APPLYING THE PRINCIPLES BACK HOME

Let me challenge you to think about the guiding principles of generativity to transforming the narratives of public education in your schools. The first principle is affirmation. This starts by capturing the historical strengths of your school district. I asked a group of Vermont central office administrators to share their stories about wanting to become educators. After two and a half hours, the twelve administrators in the room had gone through two boxes of tissues first crying and then laughing. Telling their personal stories helped them to rediscover their inspiration and passion for education. When that group looked to the future, I asked how their vision of the future had evolved over time. I asked how individually, and as a team, they might craft affirmative topics to guide their inquiry. They left refreshed and energized, and, I am told, still remembering that time together.

The second principle follows the first in establishing and expanding the affirmative topics that will guide the inquiry itself. Peters and Waterman[24] write in *In Search of Excellence* that leadership is about "nurturing good tries." Using Cooperrider and colleagues' three criteria—the main points, critical choice, and rules of thumb—challenge your district to generate a set of inquiries to chart the best way forward.

The third principle is to focus on the future. Be generative not bogged down in the present. Let's return to Donald Schön's advice: "The ways in which we set social problems determine both the kinds of purposes and values we seek to realize, and the directions in which we seek solutions." As we scan the VUCA today and think about tomorrow, what is our hope? What is our dream for our children? What makes sense in the present to prepare them for that future? Having five grandchildren, I can tell you I see possibilities I never saw for myself. These children, like their parents, have worked hard to prepare themselves for a broad range of options. They, like me, trust that with unconditional love and care, a ready ear, and counsel, they will make the right decisions about their future career and life decisions.

The fourth and final principle speaks to collaboration and connection. Here I ask educators, Can you do it alone? If not, whom do you want to work with and why? Whom do you want to bring to the table? What do you need at the table to be a successful team? How do you get others to join the mission?

The real work of leadership is about gathering others into your tent and asking them how they want to navigate the road to a desired future. The cause is noble and the work is even nobler. Without a clear purpose and core values to bind the stakeholders together, public education loses its way and chaos follows. But leaders who work and live in a world with an appreciative eye can be transformative.

# CHAPTER FIVE
## The Fifth Sphere of AO
### Managing the Paradox of Internal and External Accountability
Leonard C. Burrello

## PART ONE: ESTABLISHING INTERNAL ACCOUNTABILITY

It is a tall order to stay true to the core purposes of the school organization while managing the paradox of internal and external accountability. At each level, a relational leader must manage the politics of what people inside the school and central office see as their purpose and core values. Relational leaders gather the metrics necessary to measure progress toward them. John Mann calls this juggling act "keeping the noise out of the school" while doing what is right for students and the adults that serve them.

As I write this sphere it is becoming increasingly important that staff at all levels of the system collect and use data to inform their decision-making. Data in the form of standardized testing is contributing to a backlash from parents and teachers alike. But the era of continuous data is here, starting with classified staff generating measures to check and increase their efficiency on everything from the amount of time it takes to clean a classroom to the number of times a lesson is repeated before mastery. Professional staff used formative assessments to provide feedback to students to help them individually track progress toward their learning goals. John Mann regularly attended school meetings with teachers to discuss instructional next steps (such as increased instructional time, student groupings, and re-teaching) based on student performance data spreadsheets. State legislators are pressing superintendents to evaluate their principals and teachers using that same data.

I embraced Richard Elmore's contention that internal accountability should precede external accountability.[1] While individual educators have always had a set of internal markers to gauge their success, such as increasing reading fluency and comprehension, daily attendance, and graduation rates, what changed in the late 1980s was the rising tide of state standards and academic measures of reading and math proficiencies. This tide of reform, while state focused, was encoded in the bipartisan No Child Left Behind Act, which accelerated the curriculum (raising expectations for early reading and testing at third-, fifth-, eighth-, and eleventh-grade levels) and guaranteed students with disabilities access to the general education curriculum and classroom. These developments led Elmore to conclude in his study of a New York City community school district: "It's about instruction, instruction, and instruction."[2] In short, the shift to higher academic proficiencies and high-stakes testing meant schools had to count each and every child. This created a shift from inputs and process to outcomes and results. Instruction is the only thing a school can control. It is the learners who produce the results.[3]

In my years studying public education, it wasn't until the late 1990s that I began to see more than a few districts use formative assessments to guide instruction. I knew of even fewer districts that engaged their community stakeholders in determining what they thought was most important to measure besides academic achievement. But today, the expectation is that educators ask "What do we want to hold ourselves accountable for?" That's the essence of internal accountability.

I have witnessed many districts engage in strategic planning. My faculty and doctoral students at Indiana University observed nearly thirty-six Hoosier school districts in which, while purpose and core values might be written, it is hard to see how staff and parents are guided toward a set of goals. It was obvious that these school districts did not have agreed-upon plans for how to work toward their goal. There were mission statements on banners hanging in principals' offices and school hallways, usually shortened and transformed into slogans so they could be remembered by all. They were also painfully vague—and largely ignored because they were not measured or measurable. They left students, staff, and parents wandering the school landscape searching for a bona fide reason for being there, or as Neil Postman has suggested, searching for "an inspired reason for schooling."[4]

Educators live up to commitments expressed in purpose statements and core values by setting markers for internal assessment. The entire school community should develop these commitments and values together to be reviewed annually. At the classroom level, a simple marker for internal accountability is to ask students what they learned today. A simple question, hopefully, a parent or guardian may ask a student each night. As teachers plan and deliver daily instruction, they are accountable for determining the impact of their instruction on student learning. How do they know if and what students have learned? To gauge that impact, I have asked teachers to pause periodically and have students recall in their journals or logbooks what they recall from the day's lessons. The students can compare their individual responses to the goals for the day. A teacher could create a worksheet for students to take home asking: What have we learned? How have we helped one another? What does it mean for our learning community? Formative assessment can monitor progress at three levels: personal, classroom, and home. Three ways for three audiences to discern how well their school is living up to its commitments. For households where school is not the first order of business, this type of guide can help make school a priority, thus creating a generative conversation about learning at home.

At the school level, Larry Cuban, a retired superintendent and professor emeritus at Stanford, suggested in a Teachers College lecture series that there is no one good public school model. He asked "What makes a school a good school?" This is the question that haunts most state-level politicians in search of a magic formula to gauge school success. I contend that many politicians believe there are only a few good schools, and that those schools are largely the same with regard to their goals and how they perform.[5] Cuban suggests educators and political stakeholders ask three questions to judge a good school. I present the questions in modified form below.

1. Are students, parents or guardians, and teachers satisfied with what the students are learning through school programs and services?

2. Does the school pursue explicit goals and values directed toward student learning?

3. Does the school govern, in a democratic tradition, its planning and decision making?[6]

In his book *Flourish*, Martin Seligman challenges schools to judge how well they are adding to the well-being in their students.[7] Seligman has pilot tested the measurement of his five concepts of well-being in Australia. He suggests five measurement tasks (which I have modified for this purpose):

1. Judging the positive attitude students have toward school and work in school.

2. Judging the number of positive relationships students have with their peers and their teachers. (And are they one-way or reciprocal?)

3. Judging the degree to which students and adults are highly engaged in their learning. (To what extent do students or teachers get lost in their work?)

4. Determining the number of students who express

clear purposes for being in school. (Asking whether or not school has meaning for students in their life pursuits or career choices.)

5. Determining the breadth and depth of the students' accomplishments academically, personally, socially, and as members of the school and community.[8]

As an example, the Bartholomew County Schools in Columbus, Indiana, have developed a "senior project." Teachers and relevant community members with specific expertise are invited to help frame the project and provide resources as well as measure its clarity and impact. This is an excellent way to measure student success as well as evaluate the level of engagement the student demonstrates during the process. This is the definition of project-based learning.

Internal accountability is the lifeblood of schools and district. It is unique to each school and community; it drives daily attention to what former principal Judy Love called "keeping the main thing, the main thing." Organizations change what they study. It requires a generative learning process that involves all stakeholder groups to determine what success might be and what it looks like. How would we know it when we see it? Internal accountability measures tied to valued student outcomes, including student well-being, support continuous student and adult learning. Internal accountability precedes external accountability. It assists the leader to manage the external forces that may or may not add to your school's purpose and mission.[9]

## PART TWO: MANAGING EXTERNAL ACCOUNTABILITY

This second part of this sphere of AO addresses external accountability. The essential questions are: How do schools use external accountability as an impetus for change while not overwhelming their staff and resources? How does leadership buffer and filter external pressure for high test scores—where slipping a few percentage points ignites a crisis? How do you keep external requirements from undermining internal commitments and indicators of success?

Most school districts and schools meet external accountability pressures from federal and state mandates by doing a number of things well. This is especially true for districts with a large population of vulnerable children. In her book "It's Being Done": Academic Success in Unexpected Schools, education writer Karin Chenoweth documents what these schools are doing well.[10]

- They ensure that struggling children get the best instruction and more as needed.

- They create more instructional time and they use it wisely.

- They make decisions for the good of the children.

- They constantly re-examine what they do and what children want and are expected to learn.

- They embrace and use all the data.

- They embrace accountability both internal and external.

- They teach their students (not to a test).

- They promote an academic press and do not focus on basic skills instruction.

- They practice transparent engagement of parents and families.

- They leverage community resources.

- They are open to external scrutiny.

These "unexpected schools" calibrate what each subgroup of students needs in order to achieve proficiency, and they drive their instruction to match. They increase instructional time, observe and evaluate students every week or two, and regroup students for additional support based upon performance data. They work hard and do not give up on students. These schools are creative. They find additional time within the school day and within the school year, and use summer school to reteach students until they meet the state proficiency bar. They are open to parents and community and seek affiliations with partners who can help increase student engagement and learning outcomes. They use their talent to spread expertise among the faculty and have leadership create working conditions where all teachers and staff feel supported, valued, and respected. They build upon their strengths first.[11] Hopefully I have just described your school and its efforts to improve.

I have witnessed districts that have failed to meet the external expectations for success, and have seen the consequences of leader and teacher attrition. Changing personnel is not the only nor best solution. Buying the latest curriculum or remediation practice and installing it quickly may or may not work. The best school turnaround examples I studied in Florida and North Carolina over the past ten years build upon the positive core of the existing staff, who built capacity from the inside out. The principals I studied all started with building a critical mass of high-performing teachers who built curriculum and instruction by grade level. They hired staff who had done internships in their schools because those candidates already knew how arduous it is to meet the needs of the most vulnerable students. Superintendents created incentive programs to reward quality teaching, and most importantly, afforded school teams time to turn the school around.

When Alvin Taylor arrived in Meridian, Mississippi, the district was spending five hundred thousand dollars a year on external consultants with little to show for the investment. He took those resources and others he secured to hire a talented internal staff to move his curricular and instructional agenda forward with district leadership. The incentive program came from an external funding source and was used to award teachers who moved students academically and socially. In addition, teachers were rewarded for mentoring their peers and for providing other valuable services to the school as a whole.[12]

## TYING IT TOGETHER

Whole system coherence is embedded in internal accountability first. It requires the continual alignment of internal accountability to the district's stated purpose and core values within external pressures for success. School leaders must practice a deft hand in managing internal and external forces to determine what's most important to their system and its members.

External accountability becomes the gross measure of a school district or school's progress. Internal accountability is a formative measure of how we are going daily, weekly, monthly, and annually. Superintendent Binggeli is constantly monitoring. He reminds his district leaders they "must regularly connect their staff to the nobleness of their mission." Are we reaching the goals that we have set for students and ourselves? How are students performing? How are adults performing? The results of testing depend upon the conditions of teaching and learning regardless of the starting point. For both sets of accountability, it's all about moving students forward. And that starts in the classroom. The results reflect the quality of instruction and the depth of learning in Mr. Richardson's fourth grade or Mrs. Keen's algebra class.

In the state of Indiana, the Department of Education gave their assessments in the fall and in the late spring. Principal Judy Love feared, as did others, that the fall assessment would drive instruction toward the test itself. She told her teachers she would withhold the fall testing data because she wanted the teachers to focus on strategic instruction and high levels of student engagement instead of the state test. Principal Love managed the whole system so well, Hayden Elementary School catapulted from the bottom 20 percent in school rankings to one of the top fifty schools in the state.

# CHAPTER SIX
## The Sixth Sphere of AO
## Whole System Coherence
Leonard C. Burrello

The first five spheres operating in concert come together in the sixth sphere, whole system coherence. The first five spheres of AO—starting with creating and having a transcendent core purpose and core values—requires the ongoing work of relational leaders using a generative learning and capacity building (within a positive strengths-based) approach to innovation and change. We also argued that both the pursuit of the core purpose and the implementation of innovations and interventions put internal accountability before external accountability. Together, these five aligned spheres can lead to whole system coherence where students, staff, parents, and community contribute to a greater good.

They dynamically interact to reach the outcomes we envisioned: the connectedness of students, staff, and parents to the system, which leads to hopefulness in each participant, develops the necessary resiliency to pursue one's dreams, and finally, results in a sense of fulfillment and satisfaction with work well done. We feel better when our organization makes sense to us—when it has coherence, when it functions in a focused and integrated manner.

To cohere means to bind, to coalesce, to fuse, to stick together, and to unite for some cause or purpose. Connecting groups to a common purpose and values can lead to high levels of staff commitment. Guided by a "core ideology," people and the systems working together can achieve the explicit goals of the organization and those that individual set for themselves, or what we call internal accountability.

In these political and uncertain times, it is best when an organization's purpose is clear and bold. A bold purpose transcends the individual and challenge external demands. It inspire individuals to achieve it. Inspired reasons for schooling undergird the collective, communal focus of life in school organization.

While not an end goal itself, whole system coherence provides the means by which an end goal is reached. Whole system coherence is an essential working condition that can lead to high performance, student and adult well being, and continuous improvement. As I noted earlier, all school leaders seeking coherence in their systems and schools face the challenges of preparing students and educators to grow and to learn in the face of VUCA:

- Volatility: What new legislation is coming down the pike that will disrupt our current plans?

- Uncertainty: What will be the state's level of funding? Will we get that referendum passed this fall?

- Complexity: How can we prepare twelve hundred students to take the new state test with a new response format on our four hundred computers within the state's time frame?

- Ambiguity: How might we interpret a new mandate from the feds? What do those new rules really mean?

For example, many state legislative mandates treat all districts equally. State funding often fails to acknowledge each district's unique profile, with varying poverty levels, heaps of resources or a lack of them, ability to attract and retain quality teachers. Growing districts are rewarded, low-enrollment districts punished. It is well established that a student's zip code determines financial support as well as social capital and ultimately the potential for a high-quality post-school life and well being.

The chaotic VUCA forces require leadership to purposefully manage external expectations like high-stakes accountability and reporting requirements while delivering on internal expectations that students, parents, and teachers value more than a single test result. A hallmark of purposeful management is good communication. School leaders reassure students, staff, and parents that our purposes are worthy and merit attention. Regardless of other demands stakeholders know that the goal is preparing students for a fulfilling post-school life where they can think critically, write and speaking persuasively, demonstrate a concern for others, and do valuable and productive work. My grandson complained his fifth-grade teacher was always prepping the class to take a test or reviewing results from the last test. He was bored and unmotivated. And he went to private parochial school!

Whole system coherence requires persistent and relentless pursuit of details. The relational leader has a tall order to capture the hearts and minds of students, parents, families, and community members while managing the details of external and internal accountability.

Ultimately, we create meaning for each participant in the school community through the alignment of purpose, values, relationships, programs, and services. Whole system coherence must be driven by district and school leadership at all levels.

In the six spheres of AO framework, we identify drivers that should accrue from district and school leadership's commitment to achieving whole system coherence. This commitment should result in increases in each of these four outcomes—hopefulness, connectedness, resiliency, and fulfillment for all engaged in the life of the school, from students to faculty and staff to community members. Too few educators and fewer community members can remember a time when they heard people proclaim, "I feel connected. I know my place in this district, and my purpose." I believe that should be the rule, not the exception. Achieving district coherence starts with a comprehensible framework, like Warren Township's CORE or Meridian Compass, that is clearly articulated and visible to all stakeholders. When it comes alive, these four outcomes should be evident and observable to all.

Staff and community members must be engaged in discovering their place and contribution in the framework. It takes time and a continuous open invitation to all stakeholders to join the campaign for children. A caring and daring community will result if the foundation for results is established first and placed within a framework that has stakeholder commitment.

## CHALLENGES TO WHOLE SYSTEM COHERENCE

The challenges and/or possibilities to which Superintendents Taylor, Binggeli, and Cushenberry are responding in their districts are formidable but not insurmountable. As I reflect on the many challenges I have seen over the last thirty years of school reform, I offer below some examples that are often overlooked, ignored, or debunked.

### *I Have Been to School:* Every Perception Counts

Critics of education rarely note that because nearly everyone in our nation has attended school, most Americans assume they know what education is all about. We've all heard a people start a critique with the phrase, "When I was in school . . ." Parents are afforded the opportunity to reengage this uniquely American institution as their children march from preschool through graduation. From this vantage point, most Americans experience a second run through schools, witnessing many of the same things that made schooling work—or not work—for them. Given the political nature of public education, thoughtful observers can see how schooling is different and more challenging since their time in the lunch line. (Even the lunch line is complicated: organic produce, vegetarian options, GMOs.) But many parents aren't aware of these changes and must be reeducated to -twenty-first-century schooling with all its acronyms and technology. Many might not recognize the place.

So, school leaders face the challenge of involving parents returning to schools now as primary stakeholders. As their children pass through the system, they are moving targets. Their needs change, as the world they live in has changed.

### Fluid Participation: Changing Expectations for Students and Parents

The fluid participation in the K–12 system presents a second challenge. Adorable youngsters in new saddle shoes with superhero lunch boxes start the elementary school grade ladder, progressing from year to year. Each rung of the ladder is hopefully a gentle shift from one grade level to the next until middle school. (Actually, the progression from second to fourth grade is profound and demands excellent literacy skills.) Middle school becomes an ambiguous and uncertain place for many students as their emotional and sexual developments accelerate. While students may be physically present, their minds are spirits are often absent. They are dis-engaged. Even in exclusive Chappaqua, New York, I interviewed many students who called it a "black hole." The social dimension of middle schooling consumes a lot of energy. This adolescent evolution attempts to prepare teenagers for high school's demanding social culture (at which time parent participation falls off dramatically). In spite of all-encompassing social dimensions, middle school has the same abundance of opportunity as high school for stretching student learning, exploring occupational and career interests, and developing teamwork skills. Unfortunately, disengaged students don't usually participate effectively.

Students' worldview germinates in middle school, as do their perceptions of themselves. A school record begins that will follow them through high school. So often this record turns into a label—the geeks and jocks, the truants and dropouts. Middle school is also the pipeline to prison for students of color that starts as early as third grade. Most importantly, students' and parents' middle school experiences frame future expectations, offer (un) inspired reasons for education driven by vague goals.

Fluid participation is not only a problem for parents and students, it is increasingly a problem for district human resources departments and school-based leadership. At no time in the last fifty years has teacher and principal turnover been greater than during the last fifteen years. The external accountability demands, changing assessments, changing state targets, and new emphasis on student achievement as a measure of teacher worth have been the primary forces that have convinced many educators to walk away from their profession. Teacher and administrative retention and stability are a critical factor in maintaining system coherence.

### Achieving Equity and Excellence for All

The school's ability to achieve equity and excellence for all children is a third challenge to whole system coherence. School doors are open to students who represent all social classes, genders, races, ethnicities, sexual orientations, and (dis)abilities. Yet the system is designed to process each student the same way unless the student has behavioral or severe learning issues. Many districts view behavior and learning issues as personal pathology and use special classes or alternative schools to segregate those with disabilities, and, disproportionally, students of color. True equity requires ongoing attention to individual differences.

Columbus, Indiana has built a solid system based upon human variability within their Universal Design for Learning framework. Positive behavioral systems and the integrated school-wide reform framework of the SWIFT Center at the University of Kansas are two examples of how districts can serve all students within public schools in spite of their differences.[1]

Parent choice initiatives impact school diversity and a school district's response. In many struggling school districts, maintaining enrollments of high-achieving middle school students is a growing concern. It is not uncommon for public schools to lose their attractiveness to parents as students approach their middle and high school years. It is vital that district leadership prioritize keeping the public-ness of schools together as students transition from elementary to middle and then to high school. This requires district and school relational leaders to build strong bonds with parents and students alike. Relational leaders must frequently assess students', parents', and communities' interests in order to provide creative programming like magnet programs that engage selected stakeholders in relevant and fulfilling learning experiences.

### Accountability and Evaluation Systems: Competition or Collaboration?

Integrating new teacher and administrative evaluation systems prescribed in Race to the Top initiatives represent a fourth significant challenge to achieving whole system coherence. States were forced to implement these systems to receive an exemption (waiver) from meeting the Adequate Yearly Progress requirements of the No Child Left Behind Act of 2002–2015. Many states adopted an evaluation system based on a single test tying teacher pay to student performance. Salary levels and tenure decisions depend on these evaluations. Many of these assessments are faulty and unreliable. In many cases they do not cover the subjects taught by many teachers, particularly special area teachers. These individual student assessments provide the illusion that student performance is solely the result of classroom instruction. Such teacher assessment systems can be counterproductive and reduce the quality of teacher collaboration within grade teams and disciplines areas.

The commissioner of the state of Vermont, Rebecca Holcombe, announced in a statewide communication to parents and caregivers that the nature of federal education policy under NCLB requires that "every single school in Vermont is labeled low performing, even though many national and international measures show that Vermont is a high-performing state."[2] She explained that Vermont refused to apply for a waiver from NCLB offered by Secretary Arne Duncan, because it would have forced the state to evaluate teachers by their students' test scores. She argued that federal regulations are punitive and incoherent and that schools have purposes that are no less important (and perhaps more important) than test scores.[3] She wrote:

> We chose not to agree to a waiver for a lot of reasons, including that the research we have on evaluating teachers based on test scores suggests these methods are unreliable in classes with 15 or fewer students, and this represents about 40-50% of our classes. It would be unfair to our students to automatically fire their educators based on technically inadequate tools. Also, there is evidence suggesting that over-relying on test-based evaluation might fail to credit educators for doing things we actually want them to do, such as teach a rich curriculum across all important subject areas, and not just math and English language arts. In fact, nation-wide, we expect more and more states to give up these waivers for many of the reasons we chose not to pursue one in the first place.[4]

Holcombe's statement resonates with many educators and parents, thus fueling the backlash against testing and high-stakes accountability. Whole system coherence is threatened by direct targeting of a single group of participants in the educational system. Coherence requires balancing internal accountability with state accountability. The reaction to the first wave of these assessments has been to lower the percentage of student performance on the teacher rating system. Most states argued for 50 percent of the evaluation system to be based upon this measure; other states let local districts establish the weighing system.

## State Political Oversight: State versus Local Control / Compliance versus Innovation

The constant and ongoing state legislative activism toward public schools presents a fifth pervasive challenge to whole system coherence. Clearly education is a state function. As one local school board member suggested to me, Florida state legislators are the de facto local school board. State legislation has significantly usurped local governance, leaving local boards with less discretion, authority, and responsibility for ensuring a quality education. The tension between state activism and local district intransigency promotes compliancy and hinders innovation. Partisan politics and powerful lobbies have skewed education from a system for all to a system for select interest groups. Districts have different levels of taxing authority to generate the local revenue needed to support their schools. The allocation of state dollars across communities hinders long-range planning and the stability of school districts. State educational policies are largely regressive and chaotic— creating the oft-discussed VUCA forces. Many state policies, rules, and regulations are difficult to implement without local testing and practice to calibrate their meaning and impact. At the end of state legislative sessions lobbyists and professional associations assess the level of burdens or benefits for school stakeholders. The recent preoccupation of the Florida legislature with increasing the number of charter schools is baffling given the data we have on their limited effectiveness. In this case, the state ignores data and overrides local board decisions for nonapproval of a charter in their district. Finally, the rules governing charters are not the same as those governing the majority of public schools and districts.

Relational leadership prowess requires the successful navigation of intersecting local policy and values against the strong tide of state regulations over public schools resources and operations. Only by establishing transcendental purpose and core values can school leaders bring whole system coherence–integrating state policy mandates into their districts. Reducing local district discretion does not bode well for emphasizing internal accountability, but the overreach of the testing movement is coming home to roost in many states. The will for improvement must come through powerfully. The time is ripe for aligning external accountability measures with local measures that mean more to each community.

### Ensuring Alignment to System Values: Growing Leadership and Commitment in the Schools and Community

With AO, educators can offer alternatives to federal and state accountability mandates. If local districts can respond with reasoned and measurable indices of valued outcomes, can the state standardized testing overload and measurement be reduced as the only indicator of a quality education?

Whole system coherence is our culminating sphere. It requires constant vigilance from leadership at all levels. Professor William Foster suggested leadership is a communal property, but it starts with the commitment of those in top leadership positions to develop leaders at every level—from board members to teachers to classroom aides to bus drivers to parents and others in the community who want to contribute. They must be constantly invited to participate in school affairs and offered opportunities to lead.[5]

I chronicled Hayden Elementary School and Principal Judy Love's mission to reengage her community in the book *School Leaders Building Capacity from Within.*[6] Principal Love invited parents to come into their rural Indiana school and find ways to contribute to its success. At first, parents refused her invitations. They complained and stayed away. They had been driven away by previous administrators of the school and district. They felt devalued and excluded from the mission of the school. Principal Love went to where parents congregated, particularly the local Walmart. She went with her staff to meet with and pick up students who missed the bus. They also brought kids to school when they were sick so they could see the nurse. (Most of her students' parents worked and had no child-care available to them.) Love cared deeply for the most vulnerable students, and their parents began to believe in her. They came to believe teachers cared for their children. Teachers showed off student success in the classrooms, report card conferences, and multiple fairs at the school. Over a ten-year period the faculty grew more confident in students' taking more control over what and how they learned. Teachers' levels of collaboration increased. Principal Love asked parents to come into the schools to substitute teach for short stretches so teachers could conduct biweekly planning meetings. (It has been reported that American teachers spend significantly less time planning than teachers in high-performing nations.)[7]

The local success that occurred at Hayden Elementary was a combined effort by parents who got their children to school every day and created study time at home every night. Teachers encouraged high levels of student engagement that correlated to higher levels of student learning. Finally, the school was successful as a result of Love's creative staff, time-management strategies, and persistent invitation to staff and parents to join the movement.

Principal Love grew leadership as a means of growing the school culture. The more teacher leadership was invited, encouraged, and nurtured, the more creative thinking and ownership of organizational success took hold. Under such leadership, staff, parents, and students felt hopeful, connected, and fulfilled. Hayden was a Five Star School by the seventh year of its transformation.[8]

Keep in mind that the six spheres of appreciative organizing all move in the direction of creating whole system coherence. As Love used to say, "keeping the main thing, the main thing" is essential for all stakeholders to see how the district holds itself steady in light of the uncertainty surrounding the school and district.[9]

Another example that builds on the Indiana example is one set by the Williston School District in Williston, Vermont. I made three weeklong visits over twelve years to this K–8 elementary school, checking and rechecking the school and faculty's commitment to building a personalized learning environment for each of its students. When I first visited the school, Gary Howard, then a middle school teacher, noted that the school was not meeting the social and learning needs of two-thirds of the student population. Howard told me, "It is not very satisfying teaching the third of the students who want to be there." The school arranged its thousand students into ten teams of one hundred students within four multigrade levels. The school community was deliberately engaged in the design of curriculum. Educators, parents, and students participated in curriculum design sessions at regular intervals. Teachers organized the curriculum within two-year strands, one theme every nine weeks. For example, the fifth- and sixth-grade teams ran through eight themes in two years while their seventh- and eighth-grade counterparts ran through a different eight themes. Themes including immigration and Middle East strife for seven and eighth grade, while water resources and conservation were themes at the fifth and six grade level. Building a rich curriculum based upon community values within a project-based learning model led to the highest levels of student engagement I have every witnessed. At Williston each child pursued his or her own work with a purpose and determination that was instrumental to the school's success. This school consistently outperformed the state average. It is a model today for college and career standards curriculum development as it continues to utilize project-based learning to teach critical thinking that the new Common Core standards require.

Whole system coherence has many incarnations. Each is unique to your local community. Warren Township and Meridian, Mississippi, both developed district frameworks. At the school level, Hayden Elementary and Williston created a school-based framework with community buy-in. The former is an effective process to bring district leadership together with the board of education and the school and community at large. It's the authentic engagement of stakeholders within a positive strength-based process, focusing on how best to bring all stakeholders into the district tent. The pursuit of those explicit aspirations as measurable goals with transparent results is the process to get to whole system coherence. Always live the core values that you profess!

# AFTERWORD

## Building Positive Narratives in Public Education
## The Next Steps

Leonard C. Burrello, Linda M. Beitz, and John L. Mann

The findings of a 2014 Gallup report, "State of America's Schools: The Path to Winning Again in Education," underscores the need for a positive manifesto for public education. Gallup researchers noted "that fewer than three in ten Americans feel high school graduates are prepared for college, and that fewer than two in ten say graduates are ready to enter the labor force."[1] Research on successful schools suggests that the way out of a cycle of retribution and blame is to focus on the human elements that drive student success. Strengths development and engagement in learning are the essence of those human elements.[2] The dynamic relationships of these elements "are often overlooked in the effort to fix America's education system, but there is growing recognition that unless U.S. schools can better align learning strategies and objectives with fundamental aspects of human nature, they will always struggle to help students achieve their full potential."[3]

We agree that student well-being as defined by Seligman is the broader purpose that schools and districts need to focus on. We want to reengage the American public in narratives that tell the story of school communities coming together to support the well-being of each student. Single high-stakes test scores simply do not make exciting or inspiring stories. The why of public education needs to be rediscovered in many communities that have lost their connection to the power of school.

This book, our positive manifesto, is the first step toward

a broader mission to turn the tide on the current national discourse—a discourse that describes America's public education system as broken and desperately in need of fixing. We don't believe debating the past ills of our educational system is what's needed. We want to lend our hand in surfacing and sharing the positive, transformative narratives about schooling. We know they exist and we want to create more of them. We recognize the special challenges facing some urban and rural schools. The issues there are broader and deeper and require federal, state, and district alignment across human service agencies, economic development, and related government services. That said, every school has a success story to build upon. You can begin immediately by starting the exercises in the proceeding pages.

In the blog post "Stories as Drivers of Engagement and Innovation," AI consultant Raju Mandhyan writes:

> Stories may be truths wrapped in roses, rainbow, and rhythm, but they also create the future—that which is possible and which can indeed be beautiful. When organizations slow down or arrive at a difficult bend in their developmental journey, people within the organization need hope. They need new dreams and fresh inspiration. Success stories from the past empower us, but it is the stories into the future—stories yet to be lived—that catapult us into action and success.[4]

To capture the extant positive narratives in public education and to help others create new ones, we have created the Center for Appreciative Organizing in Education (CAOE). The CAOE is a vehicle for identifying the positive core of public education, beginning with an inquiry into what's the best of what there is and what educators want to create more of. We'll use AI best practice to inform our AO framework.

Positive narratives get co-constructed by uncovering multiple and diverse stakeholder strengths and aligning those strengths to create better schools. The process of discovery must necessarily engage large numbers of internal and external stakeholders in shaping an inspiring shared vision and set of guiding core values. Together they make up the core ideology of schooling by crafting a clear purpose and set of organizing principles for renewing school districts and schools in America's diverse communities.

We're adding to our story archive of leadership narratives and practices on our website, AOeducation.net. John writes the AO blog. As we move forward, additional training is on the horizon. A series of AO summits and newly developed partnerships—across stakeholders—from universities to businesses to other not-for-profits are on the drawing board. CAOE offers professional learning programs and advance certifications in school district redesign, appreciated educational leadership and team development, and conflict as opportunity.

This ambitious agenda will start to reverse the receding tide of support for public education. The positive core of school districts and schools will create waves of engagement in renewed educational worlds. The stakes are high. Civil society depends on it. The time is now to reimagine a uniquely American institution that endeavors to serve all students.

# A POSITIVE MANIFESTO

## NARRATIVES & EXERCISES

# NARRATIVES AND EXERCISES
## TABLE OF CONTENTS

## APPRECIATIVE INQUIRY
## WEB RESOURCES

- Appreciative Inquiry Commons, Case Western Reserve University http://appreciativeinquiry.case.edu
- Rocky Mountain Center for Positive Change http://rockymountain.positivechange.org/resources-2/
- *Appreciative Inquiry Practitioner: International Journal of Appreciative Inquiry* http://www.aipractitioner.com
- The Taos Institute http://www.taosinstitute.net/resources1
- The Center for Appreciative Inquiry http://www.centerforappreciativeinquiry.net/resources/

## 1.0 DISTRICT AI SUMMIT
## AGENDA EXERCISE
### BUILDING COMMUNITY CONFIDENCE IN DISTRICT PRINCIPLES
### CORE PURPOSES AND VALUES = CORE IDEOLOGY

A Brevard County Operating Value:
"To constantly connect people to the nobleness
of our mission"

The purpose of this activity is twofold: first to build public confidence in your public schools' purpose and operation, and second, to acknowledge the benefits the district brings to the community. To accomplish this, you need a broad coalition of school and community representatives engaged in the conversation. The appreciative or affirmative question to ask stakeholders is, How can our public schools serve the whole community so everybody can share in their success? What should drive our work with students in this community? Why it is important? The answers to these and other questions will coalesce into an action plan to guide the school district's work to the benefit of the community, school professionals, and most importantly, the students.

## AN EXAMPLE: MERIDIAN PUBLIC SCHOOL DISTRICT TWO-DAY SUMMER ADVANCE
### Objectives for an Educational Summit

1. Using a strengths-based approach, cocreate a district framework to build whole system coherence.

2. Establish district priorities related to our purpose(s) and core values and informed by current data to be translated into goals and work groups.

3. Test the framework through five work groups to drive decision making at all levels of the system.

4. Endorse and share plan with the board, professional and classified staff, and the community at large.

## CONTEXT: VOLATILITY, UNCERTAINTY, COMPLEXITY, AND AMBIGUITY (VUCA)
### Three Assumptions Underpinning Our Work

1. Schools/districts need clear purposes and core values, not long-term strategic plans but specific flexible action plans

2. School transformation needs to be equity based and change social conditions

3. The questions we ask and our ability to imagine/ articulate the future we want to see will determine the change we make happen

## AGREEMENTS TO MOVE WORK FORWARD

- Value each and all perspectives
- Acknowledge the individuality of language when discussing the issue
- Rely upon data sources that contribute to understanding the issue
- Commit to reaching consensus through shared understanding in the group
- The collective impact is greater than the individual impact
- Move on specific actionable goals
- Stay affirmative and remember the nobleness of our mission to children

## SOAR

Strengths, Opportunities, Aspirations, and Results (SOAR) is a vehicle to discuss desired futures, core values, strengths, and a collective commitment to common district goals. (Meridian used the SOAR framework to guide the conversation.)

### SOAR Questions

#### Strengths:

- What are we really doing well?
- What are our greatest assets?

#### Opportunities:

- How do we frame and see the future?
- What are our aspirations?
- Who should we become?

#### Results:

- What matters?

## SOAR COMPARED TO OTHER ORGANIZATIONAL DEVELOPMENT PROCESSES

- Action not analysis oriented
- Strengths and opportunity focused, not weakness and threats focused
- Possibility focus, be the best, noncompetitive, just get better
- Innovation and breakthroughs, not incremental improvement
- Engagement of all levels not top down
- Focus on planning to implementation not analysis to planning
- Energy creating not energy depleting
- Attention to results not gaps

## PLAN FOR DAY ONE: FOUR STEPS

**Step One**—Group Storytelling and Share

Ask: What prepared you for what you do?

**Step Two**—Identify Story Themes

**Step Three**—Brainstorming for 2027 and Rapid Prototyping Exemplars

Ask: How can we mining our stories to determine how to reframe in order to see the opportunities for our students in 2027

How do we allow our values to drive our vision of the future for our students?

**Step Four**—Translating Desired Futures into a District Framework

Ask: What do we want to be known for?

## PLAN FOR DAY TWO: FIVE STEPS

Ask: How can we make a difference for Meridian schools?

**Step One**—Review previous day's work. Make revisions that are inclusive of the leadership group

**Step Two**—Share current data on the state of the district and establish clear or emerging targets

**Step Three**—Establish goals, work groups, and an action plan

Clarify group leaders, expectations, membership, time line, and progress monitoring protocol

**Step Four**—Determine district and school nonnegotiable issues

**Step Five**—Draft a clear message for this work

# 1.1 MAPPING THE ROOT CAUSES OF SUCCESS EXERCISE
## EXERCISE COURTESY OF WARREN TOWNSHIP SUPERINTENDENT DENA CUSHENBERRY, POWERPOINT DEVELOPED MEGAN TRIERWEILER

### OVERVIEW

This exercise examines crucial life circumstances that have impacted you as a leader. Brainstorm a list and consider how each circumstance has rooted your leadership philosophy. Write a belief statement. Next, establish a leadership principle that you believe is fundamental to leadership behavior and is manifested in your practice as a district or school.

Review Superintendent Cushenberry's example and Go Fishing with a colleague to build your own fish bone of root causes of your success. We've included slides from Cushenberry.

Charting the Course: Life Circumstances, Root Cause(s), Insights, Belief System, Principles.

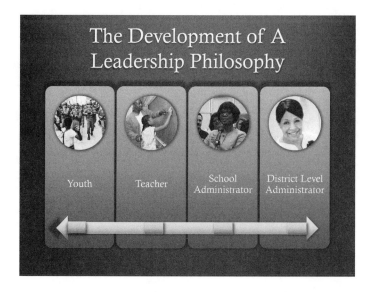

The Development of A Leadership Philosophy

Youth | Teacher | School Administrator | District Level Administrator

## YOUTH

Describe one or two life circumstances / experience that shaped your values. And then, ask yourself:

- What was at the root of this experience that made it valuable?

- What other insights do you have about this?

- What part of your belief system did this experience highlight or help develop?

- How does this translate into a general principle you now hold?

# Youth

| Life Circumstance: Childhood in Denver, CO 1960's | | | |
|---|---|---|---|
| **Root Cause** | **Insights** | **Belief System** | **Principles** |
| • Race Riots<br>• Death<br>• Drugs | • Developed Resiliency<br>• Helped Mother | • Create alternative views<br>• Could be a role model | • Understanding others<br>• Student can overcome disadvantages |

| Life Circumstance: Early Adolescence and Peer Pressure | | | |
|---|---|---|---|
| **Root Cause** | **Insights** | **Belief System** | **Principles** |
| • Jealous/ Threatening Peers<br>• Supporting Family w/ Job | • Questioning status quo<br>• Fend for yourself<br>• Finding Mentors | • Expect something more<br>• Faith<br>• Seeing outside environment | • Creating a new worldview<br>• Lifelong service |

## TEACHER

Continue your story by describing your first teaching position (life circumstances).

- What was at the root of this experience that made it valuable?

- What other insights do you have about this?

- What part of your belief system did this experience highlight or help develop?

### Teacher

| Life Circumstance: Teacher of Student with Significant Disabilities | | | |
| --- | --- | --- | --- |
| Root Cause | Insights | Belief System | Principles |
| • Focus on student interest/ motivation | • Personalizing Learning<br>• Empathy for Parents | • All students are valued | • All children have the right to pursue multiple life goals |
| Life Circumstance: Assistant Director of Special Education | | | |
| Root Cause | Insights | Belief System | Principles |
| • Advocating for special needs in mainstream | • Everyone needs an advocate<br>• System preferences ≠ Best for all | • Public Ed must include ALL | • Work from stakeholder perspective- not our own |

## SCHOOL ADMINISTRATOR

Continue your story by describing your first administrative position (life circumstances).

- What was at the root of this experience that made it valuable?

- What other insights do you have about this?

- What part of your belief system did this experience highlight or help develop?

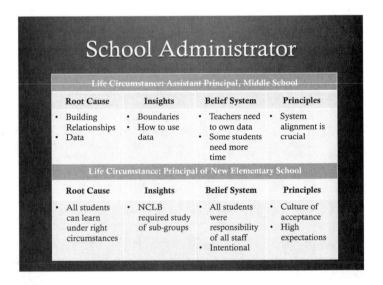

### School Administrator

#### Life Circumstance: Assistant Principal, Middle School

| Root Cause | Insights | Belief System | Principles |
|---|---|---|---|
| • Building Relationships<br>• Data | • Boundaries<br>• How to use data | • Teachers need to own data<br>• Some students need more time | • System alignment is crucial |

#### Life Circumstance: Principal of New Elementary School

| Root Cause | Insights | Belief System | Principles |
|---|---|---|---|
| • All students can learn under right circumstances | • NCLB required study of sub-groups | • All students were responsibility of all staff<br>• Intentional | • Culture of acceptance<br>• High expectations |

## DISTRICT ADMINISTRATOR

- How does the typical hierarchy of leadership work or fail to work?

- How does changing the perspective impact teaching and learning?

- How does Dr. Cushenberry's story illustrate this point?

- In your view, how does this work in your district?

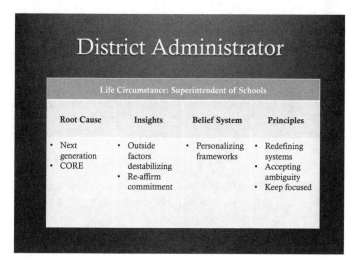

**District Administrator**

| Life Circumstance: Assistant Superintendent for C & I | | | |
| --- | --- | --- | --- |
| **Root Cause** | **Insights** | **Belief System** | **Principles** |
| • Data rich environment<br>• Vertical improvement-Elm to MS | • Rebalance district ethnically/racially | • Changing dynamics | • Equity in search of excellence |

| Life Circumstance: Deputy Superintendent | | | |
| --- | --- | --- | --- |
| **Root Cause** | **Insights** | **Belief System** | **Principles** |
| • Having mentors<br>• Moving an entire school | • Data became key | • Right people, right place<br>• Academic and Social<br>• Student Voice | • Monitoring Values<br>• Challenge status quo |

**District Administrator**

| Life Circumstance: Superintendent of Schools | | | |
| --- | --- | --- | --- |
| **Root Cause** | **Insights** | **Belief System** | **Principles** |
| • Next generation<br>• CORE | • Outside factors destabilizing<br>• Re-affirm commitment | • Personalizing frameworks | • Redefining systems<br>• Accepting ambiguity<br>• Keep focused |

## DISTRICT ADMINISTRATOR

- How does Dr. Cushenberry's story illustrate a theory of action of district-wide improvement?

- In your view, how does this work in your district?

## **1.2 TIME TO GO FISHING!**

**Follow the example of Dr. Cushenberry's story.**

1. You and a partner identify your root causes of success.

2. Fill in your own "fish bone" chart.

3. Ask: How can pinpointing this information help improve your practice?

4. Share your results with colleagues.

5. Develop an action plan to implement new discoveries.

Cushenberry's Fish Bone Chart

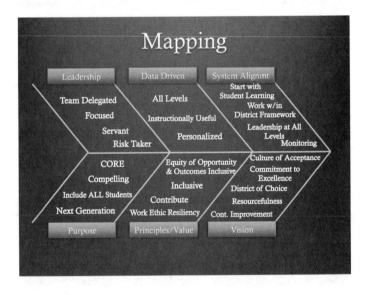

# 3.0 TALE OF TWO PRINCIPALS

Consider the two stories of leaders. Look for traits that you have observed in others. Remember that while it is better to learn from positive examples we can and must learn from nonexamples as well. While reading these scenarios think of ways to use the stories as well as the information to build and improve as relational leaders.

## EXAMPLES OF RELATIONAL LEADING

## A TALE OF TWO PRINCIPALS

### The First Story

The same rollout of a new district initiative was handled two different ways in two different schools. Principal Smith and Principal Jones are interesting stories, with one being more fortunate than the other. Ms. Smith was the principal of the Contentious School, and Ms. Jones was the principal of the Respectful School. Each principal had a faculty meeting scheduled for the day following her district meeting. A new district initiative contained an emphasis on different teaching strategies than most of the teachers were currently using. Bits and pieces of information had been getting out to the teachers before the principals were briefed as a group on what might be expected. The antithesis of a hopeful leader is the principal who comes back to school after a briefing on a new district initiative and does the following: Principal Smith cancels the agenda for the school faculty meeting the next day. She takes the information straight from her briefing and doesn't share it with anyone. She does not prepare for the staff meeting, because why should she do that since she is just going to read the information word for word and send the staff on their way. Principal Smith arrives the next morning at the meeting and is completely disgusted with the whole process and situation. She does nothing to make the environment more welcoming. Her disgust shows on her face and is reflected in her body position. Her voice is monotone with no hint of emotion. She stands up in front of the group with her arms crossed and reads the information about the new initiative aloud. She states that she does not have any more details and isn't sure how it will work out. When the staff asks questions she replies that this is all she knows but it is their job to carry out this new directive starting next week. She will scan a copy of the information and send it out to their department chairs when she gets a chance. She then dismisses the group from the meeting. Now, you can imagine how this works out. The gossip and phone lines are burning up. Time spent on the rollout: less than one hour. Success for students from the new information: next to nothing. Harm to the organization: irreparable.

Principal Smith had no confidence in her ability to implement initiatives successfully at the Contentious School. She was unwilling to give the proper time and attention to a careful implementation. Her lack of knowledge of the change process and her lack of confidence in her abilities became apparent when she abdicated her leadership responsibility and control and created a negative culture with no chance of success.

**The Second Story**

Principal Jones was in the same briefing as Principal Smith. Principal Jones sits at a different table than Principal Smith because she does not like the tenor of negative conversation at the table where Principal Smith sits. Principal Jones was not completely happy with the way the district official shared the new information. She had some previous knowledge of what was coming from volunteering to work on a district committee during the summer. She had started to transition her school in the direction the district was suggesting because of the research that she was doing and her work with one of the school's Professional Learning Communities. When the meeting was over, she contacted her assistant principal and curriculum specialist. She gave them an overview and asked if they could come to school an hour early the next day so they could discuss what they were going to share with the faculty at the meeting. She also asked them to add an agenda item so they could briefly share some information they were sure would help the faculty in the future. She believed that a clear, well-thought-out plan was the best approach if they were going to have any success. While Principal Jones was in the district briefing, she spent the entire time looking for the positives within the presentation. She made notes to tie the new initiative to current work and practices at the school (even if that work was not being done by every teacher).

The next morning she met with the assistant principal and curriculum specialist as planned. The three of them would become the core of the Guiding Coalition to further this work in the school successfully. The assistant principal and curriculum specialist helped Principal Jones think through what she was going to share and decided that she would take about five minutes in the meeting to discuss what she had learned. They had refreshments and a time for sharing accomplishments on the three major school development projects. They had a specific time reserved to thank fellow staff members for being helpful and kind. When it came time for sharing new information, the principal stood, looked out, and declared how proud she was to be a part of such an amazing and caring group of professionals. She reminded them that, as was demonstrated today by reports and moments of gratitude, the new initiative would be a whole school effort. It could not be accomplished without the concerted effort of teachers, specialists, and all of the instructional support personnel. She then shared that she knew there had been some discussion throughout the district and within their school about a different focus for instruction being proposed by the district. She assured them that it was nothing to be alarmed about. As a school, they were already working on many of the items that were discussed in her meeting. She shared a couple of those examples. She then stated her confidence in their existing plans for the year and expectation that they would continue the good work that was already happening on behalf of the students. She pointed out that, as demonstrated that morning in the reports, they knew what they were doing and where they were going. With that being said, as a progressive school they always welcomed the opportunity to explore their own practices and expand their knowledge. They would be doing this with the district's assistance in the future. They would not be changing direction at this time but would start the careful planning and professional development, as per their normal protocols for assisting the school as it moved forward.

Although some of this was new for her, she believed in the protocols at Respectful School and knew beyond a shadow of a doubt they would be successful with implementation after careful planning. She knew they would because many times in the past they had been successful. As you might guess, Principal Jones had a huge smile and an open body posture. She radiated confidence, love, and respect for the entire faculty.

### Review of Principal Smith and Jones Thoughts

In her mind, Principal Smith was done with the rollout for the Contentious School. She was told that they were going to be moving forward in this new direction, and so she told the staff that this was the way it was going to be. No need to waste any more time and effort on something about which you have no choice. Principal Jones at the Respectful School heard the same message as Principal Smith but used a completely different filter. She would not do something that was not in the very best interest of the children if at all possible. She was determined to find the very best in the new initiative. She believed that, although it may have been presented poorly, good could be found in most well-intentioned initiatives. It was her job to find it and to protect her staff from the hysteria that surrounded inappropriate rollouts of new initiatives. She understood the research and believed that her staff would do an excellent job with this new work, just as they had with all of their work.

Principal Smith, as you might expect, bombed in her work at the Contentious School and in leading in general. The school implemented the new district initiative very poorly and had to have intervention from the district with professional development and assistance dealing with the union. Their efforts were considered some of the worst in the district. Principal Smith retired from education after just two years as a principal. Principal Jones at the Respectful School led the school through a complete process of positive implementation, during which time she gained a clear picture of exactly what a successful conclusion to their new work would look like and why it was crucial. They leaned on the research as well, considering the personal interests, learning styles, and levels of proficiency of the staff. They attempted to include as much autonomy as possible while embracing an inquiry approach. Although the rollout was not without some bumps, the entire school pitched in and worked through it together. In two years, they were considered the model for the district and had increased their achievement scores at an even greater rate than before. The principal stayed at the school for many years, as did a great many of the staff.

## Principal Jones Reflections

Principal Jones at the Respectful School was building relational capital as she was leading the school. She was hopeful, even though in the case of the new initiative she could not present a clear and confident picture of what success looked like. She was able to be hopeful in the process and school protocols that had produced success in the past. She demonstrated honesty when she stated that they still had work to do on the new initiative. Staff members showed gratitude for one another when they thanked each other and praised one another's work. Competence was shown in the school development reports and success was celebrated.

As you start to think about this simple twenty-four-hour time frame, you can clearly see how much relational capital Principal Jones built up in a short amount of time. Principal Jones took every chance possible to increase the ratios of positives to negatives in the dialogue within the school. She did this through the positive and hopeful nature of her conversations. She also did her best to be a true model of hopefulness, honesty, kindness, caring, trustworthiness, motivation, and respectfulness. None of this would have worked if something had been out of synch. If her expressions had not been in line with her words, people would not have reacted as well. If she had not proved trustworthy in the past, then some would have doubted her. If they had heard of her discussing staff members in a disrespectful way in a more private setting or on social media, then her actions would have betrayed her intentions. She was extremely successful because she kept the building blocks of relational capital in mind and lived by them in all situations. They created the foundation for her success.

### Reflections

What can we learn from this small glance into the Respectful School? Ask yourself under what conditions does a staff work best. How does the leader develop hope for the staff? Did the leader establish goals, a reasonable way to meet those goals, and belief that the staff could change and grow to meet the goals? Think about the questions for a moment.

We cannot always control the way the landscape changes from external forces, but we can change the way we react. We can determine how we will process the information and share it with our stakeholders. The goal is to meet the needs of students through their interaction with compassionate human beings. Raising student achievement is always the goal, but doing it while raising staff and student morale is a moral imperative. Spend time daily developing character—for you, your staff, and your students. Your attitude defines your perception of a situation or an event. If you are coming to a situation believing that it cannot possibly work out, then you are correct. Henry Ford said it best: "Whether you think you can or think you can't—you're right." We believe it easy for all of us to understand the effect of one's attitude on our two schools and their situation. When in doubt remember Martin Seligman's ABC model. It holds that beliefs (B) about an adversity (A)—and not the adversity itself—cause consequent (C) feelings.[1] Our thoughts, attitudes, and beliefs about situations drive our actions. When times get tough, always remember the ABCs.

## 3.1 VISIONING EXERCISE

Purpose and Reminders: The purpose is to practice and sharpen our skills at clearly seeing a positive future that we believe is most beneficial for our organization. In the exercise we start with small things and each person can quickly add to the list of possibilities. The future we envision will reflect our positive attitude and belief about the possibility of tremendous success. Our attitude will be the tiller that steers our vision. This exercise is designed to help you to further your most positive work. Do not get caught in a negative cycle and let your vision forecast a future of doom and gloom. Stay positive. Practicing and envisioning a positive outcome does not take away those surprises that each leader will encounter. It places more importance on the possibilities rather than being driven from moment to moment by whatever happens next.

**Step 1**—Get Started: Take five minutes in a quiet place to practice your visioning skills.

A. See the event clearly in your mind's eye. (Sometimes it may help to close your eyes.)

B. After you can clearly see the event, listen in to what people are saying when your event is going its best.

**Step 2**—Participate in your vision: After you have carried out your vision exercise, go out and participate in the event that you envisioned. Many times athletes have stated that the events that they envisioned happened in a very similar way to their vision.

**Step 3**—Take notes about the success that you found in step 2 and how close it was to what you envisioned in step 1.

## 3.2 COMMUNICATING A POSITIVE IMPRESSION EXERCISE

Take time during your commute to envision a positive entrance into the office, team, or department.

**Step 1**—Envision:

A. Who you see

B. What the environment looks like

C. What you will say

D. How people will react to your smile and positive body language

E. What you hear going on

**Step 2**—You are getting ready to do a walk-through (flyover) of the school, team, or department. Take time in your office or room to prepare for a helicopter view of all the areas that you will be observing. Envision:

A. Begin from your starting point and go slowly down the route that you will be taking. Ceilings and roofs are pulled back for you so there are no obstacles.

B. See people that you will greet. Observe the way people react to your smile and friendly greeting. See yourself smiling and greeting people in a very positive manner.

C. If in a school, go into the classroom and see and hear children and teachers at their best. (Adjust for your work environment.)

D. See and hear yourself interacting with people. Listen to how you are encouraging them with specific praise. You are adding to the positive ratio of comments for the person's day.

E. In your mind finish your walk-through (flyover) in a positive manner.

**Step 3**—You are preparing for a meeting or presentation. Envision:

A. The environment

B. The materials you will use

C. Being confident because of your planning

D. Hearing your opening remarks

Tips: See and hear yourself being open and welcoming with your body position, expressions, and word choice. Anticipate the audience's response.

# 3.3 EVERYONE CAN HEAR MY THOUGHTS EXERCISE

Purpose and Reminders: The purpose is to be your most genuine and honest self. The term *transparent* has been overused, but it fits in this exercise. You will envision that the person in your meeting, presentation, or personal exchange can hear not only your words but your thoughts. Are our thoughts and words congruent? The research is very interesting—it suggests that we cannot easily have a convincing discussion if we believe something entirely different from what we are saying. Our expressions generally give us away. How would you treat people if they could hear your thoughts? Practice this exercise in transparency.

**Step 1**—Think about an upcoming meeting, presentation, or personal exchange.

**Step 2**—Think about what you going to say.

**Step 3**—Think about why you are going to say what you are preparing to say.

**Step 4**—Is what you are going to say congruent with what you believe? If the person(s) in the conversation or presentation were able to hear your thoughts, would that be a positive thing?

**Step 5**—Change, if necessary, what you are saying in order to accomplish the same goals while keeping in mind your personal beliefs about what is correct and right. Can you say what you need to say with someone hearing your thoughts?

# 3.4 LEGACY EXERCISE

Purpose and Reminders: This exercise can be completed no matter the stage of your career. It helps to find a quiet place to think about the things that you believe are most important in life. Often parents will say that they want their children to be happy, healthy, and to have a good life. When asked about what they want from their child's education it is much simpler, to learn their core subjects and/or to be ready for college. You can do better than that as you describe your legacy.

**Step 1**—Write a paragraph about your last day at work in your current job as you prepare to retire or move to a new assignment.

**Step 2**—Think about what people are saying about you as you leave when you cannot hear them. Try to hear their words and feel the emotion of what they are saying.

**Step 3**—Consider the things that you can control and do not depend on an occurrence of blind luck.

**Step 4**—Place the piece of paper in an envelope in your desk. (This can be done on your computer, and you can make adjustments as you grow and develop.)

# 3.5 SMILE TRIAL EXERCISE

Purpose and Reminders: This is a powerful but simple exercise. You will be amazed at the response of the people within your organization. This must be a genuine smile that involves your entire face, not just curling your lips up. That can be scary. Your goal is to consciously smile and greet every person that you meet for one week. It is good if you have someone who is doing it with you so that you can share your findings from the trial. At the end of each day you will need to record your discoveries.

**Step 1**—Start your preparation on the way to work. Remind yourself of your goal of smiling at every person that you meet that day and share an appropriate greeting.

> Tip: Practice in the mirror and start to think about all the amazing things about your team, department, or organization that make you proud.

**Step 2**—Use a ring, bracelet, or rubber band as a reminder of your trial.

**Step 3**—Start with the first person and watch for people's reactions.

**Step 4**—At the end of the day, record the best quote, inquiry, or reaction.

**Step 5**—Continue the trial when you get home. (Everyone deserves your best.)

## 3.6 ASKING QUESTIONS EXERCISE

Purpose and Reminders: The purpose is to further our relationship building with staff and to open the doors to many important opportunities to support and assist individuals, teams, departments, and organizations. Asking positive strength-based questions influences every situation in which we find ourselves. This question could be asked of an individual about his or her own work or a group about their project. It should be clear what type of assistance you are willing to supply, and then you must be willing to act on the things that you commit to. Never insinuate that you are willing to do things that you are not going to follow through on. The *Encyclopedia of Positive Questions* by Diana Whitney, David

L. Cooperrider, Amanda Trosten-Bloom, and Brian S. Kaplan is a great reference. You can add any question that might be helpful to you and your organization in Step 1.

Promises kept from a single innocent question:

**Step 1**—Ask the question "How might I help you?" (It might start with "I know that you are working hard on (fill in the blank) and I was wondering . . .")

**Step 2**—Listen intently to the answer.

**Step 3**—Give your full attention and do not interrupt.

**Step 4**—Ask probing questions with the full intent of getting the person you are speaking to talk more about their work or situation.

**Step 5**—Decide if there is any way that you are able to assist them beyond listening.

**Step 6**—Provide specific verbal praise and positive reinforcement as appropriate.

**Step 7**—Only commit to what you are willing to do.

**Step 8**—Write down and schedule the follow up to anything that you commit to do.

**Step 9**—Keep a list on your calendar of whom you have met with and make a commitment to meet with each staff member by a specific date. (Work through the entire staff over a set time.)

**Step 10**—Take action. (The action could be as simple as a follow-up meeting or providing some additional funding. It should not include you doing the work yourself.)

# 3.7 GRATITUDE EXERCISE

Purpose and Reminders: Gratitude improves our mental outlook about our day, week, and year. This exercise is about getting your own thinking aligned in the right direction. We must remember the good in our lives in an appreciative way to create the most positive personal position. Work on this exercise for at least thirty days.

**Step 1—**Determine where the most appropriate place is for you to keep your gratitude log. (Sometimes people keep it in their calendar, but it does not matter where you keep it, as long as you have easy access.)

**Step 2—**At the end of the workday, write down the three things that you are most grateful for on that day. Tip: You may add things that you are grateful for at home but remember to record at least three items from work.

**Step 3—**First thing in the morning, before you go to work or as soon as you get to your desk, review your gratitude log from the previous day. (It is perfectly okay to look at more than one day, but make sure that you look at the previous day's log.)

**Step 4—**Make a statement of positive affirmation: "Just as yesterday had many important aspects for which I am grateful, so will today. This is going to be a great day, and my list of things for which I am grateful will be different but very positive."

**Step 5—**At the end of one week, two weeks, three weeks, and four weeks, write a short statement about how keeping your gratitude log has helped you.

# 3.8 SAY THANK YOU EXERCISE

Purpose and Reminders: The purpose of this exercise is to get to all members of your team, department, school, or organization with the sole purpose of saying thank you to as many people as possible. Go out of your way to thank two different people on your staff each day for something big or small that they did to help the staff, department, customers, or organization. This has to be sincere and delivered personally to them. You can e-mail or call staff members with good things but, if you are on the physical property, you must deliver it to them in person.

**Step 1**—Determine whom you are going to thank on a specific day and what you are going to thank them for. Tip: The more specific, the better, and the more it will mean to them. This is not a time when you just say thank you. It must be about how much you appreciate the specific thing they did or achieved. Everyone has something that they can be thanked for in a sincere manner.

**Step 2**—Keep a log of whom you have met with so that you get to everyone over time.

**Step 3**—Do not stop until you have gotten to every person at least one time.

**Step 4**—When you have completed the exercise, record some of the amazing things that have occurred or you have learned because of the simple act of sincerely thanking someone for something they did.

# 4.0 GENERATIVE QUESTIONS AND ACTION EXERCISE
## THE RELENTLESS PURSUIT OF READING LITERACY

A principal and her third-grade teachers are going to a district meeting after the superintendent presented the recent December proficiency scores of all third-grade readers to the entire district. The news media has picked the story up, and the consequence for almost all children not passing the third-grade test will be mandatory retention for one year, two years of retention for students with disabilities and ELL students. New state legislation is pending. Only two schools either approached the 51 percent level of proficiency at the third grade or exceeded it. Your school was particularly low in reading with only 32 percent of your students at proficiency, and your math scores were even lower, at 28 percent.

The assistant superintendent for curriculum and instruction will lead the meeting and expects that you and your teachers will add at least one hour to your current ninety-minute reading block for all students and provide additional time on reading across its five dimensions from fluency to comprehension for your targeted red flashing students, your yellow cautionary students, and your blue achieving students. She will also recommend using your best teachers to teach the red students, lowering student/teacher ratios. She recommends assessing their progress over the next fifteen days, and prepare to discuss student progress at the grade level team meeting.

Using the example above for a proficient third-grade reader, what generative questions would you put in place? What would be the nature of the generative conversation? What initial generative actions might evolve?

Here is a blown-out example and a sample form for your use on an affirmative topic you wish to promote locally.

# FORM COMPLETED FOR THE PREVIOUS EXAMPLE:

| LEVEL OF EFFORT AND FOCUS: GENERATIVE AND AN AFFIRMATIVE TOPIC: AN IMAGE OF A PROFICIENT THIRD-GRADE READER | | | |
|---|---|---|---|
| | Generative questions | Generative conversations | Generative actions |
| For Students | Why is setting a goal in reading helpful for you? | What do you want to know and learn about? What you already know about the subject or topic? | How might one go about selecting a book, magazine, or newspaper, or an online article? How does one know if the goal has been met? How might we measure our success? |
| Teacher–Student Relationships | Why are teachers important? Why is it important to agree on the way we talk to one another? | What does trust and respect for one another mean? What are each of us trying to get out of school? | How do we get the best out of one another? |
| Classroom | Why is reading important for everyone? | What are the range of topics we all want to learn about in this classroom? | How might we organize our goals and our topics? How will we celebrate each week when we reach our goals? |
| School | Why do we come to school each day? Why is it important? | What do we like about school? | How are we successful in school? |

| Parent/ Community Partnerships | Why do your parents send you to school each day? | What do your parents say about school? What do your parents want you learn each day? | How will we tell your parents about school each day? By 2:30 each day what can you write about how successful you were each day? |
| --- | --- | --- | --- |
| | | | |

## SAMPLE FORM FOR LOCAL USE:

| Level of Effort and Focus | Generative Topic/ Affirmative Topic/ Image | Generative questions | Generative conversations | Generative actions |
| --- | --- | --- | --- | --- |
| Student | | | | |
| Teacher–Student Relationship | | | | |
| Classroom | | | | |
| School | | | | |
| District | | | | |
| Parent/Community Partnership | | | | |
| Other relationships of interest | | | | |

As you review projects that you are engaged in presently you might use this example to recast your topics as affirmative topics first and then generative images of them. What might the images look like, say, and suggest them to your working colleagues? What are three or four generative questions that encourage a deep dive into the image, its value, meaning, and context? Imagine the conversations you would hope might emerge from your questioning. What generative actions are you seeking to move your conversation from talk to implementing concrete action toward your image of the future? Consider a move to roll out the work over the next two or three years, how will you sustain the work and maintain the energy and commitment to our mutual goals?

# 6.0 MEASURING DISTRICT WELL-BEING
## EXERCISES LEADING TO WHOLE SYSTEM COHERENCE

We think measuring the well-being of staff, students, parents, or guardians is a key activity within an appreciative organization in public education. We offer well-being as a purposive goal of school districts. It requires measures of internal accountability to determine success. When we were rolling out the district Compass and set of actions plans for the Meridian School District in Meridian, Mississippi, to all staff, both professional and classified, a classified staff member asked me: "Are we to be invisible in this process?" I quickly turned to his supervisor, a member of the fifty-two-person district planning team, and asked him: How will you continue to include the voices and perspectives of your staff during the implementation of the Compass? What might be your staff's level of engagement? Could an e-mail update to all internal and external parties be distributed monthly or quarterly? I suggested at least one face-to-face meeting of all staff subgroups annually. This meeting would be used to enable the continued flow of information and data on district fidelity assessments on all district goals and work group recommendations, and would be the backbone of the district's annual report to the Board of Education. In the end, the superintendent proposed a semiannual congregation of all parties be considered to maintain a direct connection with all staff.

We recommended that all work of the district be subject to fidelity measures to ensure progress monitoring toward the district goals. But this also maintains a transparent system of communication that relies on extant data that the district collects filtered through the lived experience of all staff in the district. All measures and data can be correlated with the five measures Martin Seligman recommends.

Answer the guiding questions below to measure fidelity toward Seligman's five dimensions of well-being, and the four drivers of whole system coherence: Hopefulness, Connectedness, Resiliency, and Fulfillment.

> **1.** Positive disposition toward school and work. Do I look forward to going to work and making my contribution to our mission? Is my attendance excellent? Am I encouraged to do good work? Do I find my work fulfilling?
>
> **2.** Relationships. Are my colleagues helpful and thoughtful and considerate of my voice and perspective? Do they respect and trust me to do a good job? Do I have meaningful communication with my coworkers and with my department leader?
>
> **3.** Engagement. Am I fully engaged in my work? Am I empowered to make decisions on my own? Do I get lost in my work? Am I persistent because I think our work is important and meaningful?
>
> **4.** Purpose and Meaning. Do I know my purpose here and how it contributes to the mission of the district or school? Do I do valuable work in this district and/or school? Do I believe my work leads add to my fulfillment?  Do I believe my work is impacting student learning, and/or the culture of the district and schools?
>
> **5.** Accomplishment. In what ways am I achieving the results that I have set for myself? How do I identify what

I have achieved each day and feel good about it? Does my department leader let me know that I have done a good job? Are others better off because I am here, if so, in what ways?

## 6.1 MANAGING INTERNAL AND EXTERNAL ACCOUNTABILITY

As stated in the opening paragraph to chapter six, getting to whole system coherence is complex and elusive. The complexity includes state and federal assessments of student learning by subgroup, reducing achievement gaps, graduate rates, teacher and principal quality, and fiscal responsibility for the expenditure of public resources.

Richard Elmore was the first to argue in 1990's, then Michael Fullan, that internal accountability should precede external accountability. The state takeover of student and teacher assessment is a new phenomenon and like most state policy is a crude instrument that is not attuned to local contexts and circumstances. A single annual assessment by which to judge both groups performance is a narrow and limited measure of quality. The problem today is that most educators feel misaligned with state policy, and their discretion is largely reduced to teaching to the test since so much is resting on the consequences for their students and themselves. We think the data on school transformation suggests that internal accountability is a better index to judge a good school or district, as Cuban also suggested.

In this exercise, have your district or school level teams identify both internal or external accountability initiatives, identify their source, whether or not they are compatible and can be used for multiple purposes or should be singularly focused. Finally, ask team members to identify the stakes attached to the measure: high, medium, or low. Keeping an ongoing initiatives listing attached to the district or school's core ideology—purpose and core values— and identifying the relative importance of the stakes attached to each, helps flesh out the pressure to perform and the consequences that might accrue for students, their families, staff, the school as a whole, and the district.

| Initiative and Source | Internal Accountability Standard | External Accountability Standard | Compatible Incompatible Additional | Accountability Stakes—High, Medium, or Low |
|---|---|---|---|---|
| College and Career Readiness Standards State/Federal Accountability Measures | Preparedness | To what extent achieved | Compatible | High |
| Graduation Rates State/Federal Accountability Measures | Successful credit accumulation tied to local and state programming | Percentage graduated | Compatible | High |
| Reduce achievement gaps between subgroups of students State/Federal Accountability Measures | Increased proficiency of each subgroup Race/Ethnic ELL SWD | Percentage narrowed | Compatible | High |
| Student and Staff Well-being Local Discretion | Five criteria | No counterpart | Additional | Low |

| Senior Legacy Projects Local Discretion | Local criteria established | Percentage of projects completed, defended, and rated as excellent by community panels of stakeholders and experts | Additional | Moderate |
|---|---|---|---|---|
| | | | | |

Once you have completed this matrix, prioritize your internal and external responses to each accountability indices and ask if they are the ones that you want to pursue and measure fidelity to for an ongoing assessment of the enactment of your values.

# NOTES

## Foreword

1   Marge Schiller, *Exceeding Expectations: An Anthology of Appreciative Inquiry Stories in Education from Around the World* (Chagrin Falls, OH: Taos Institute, 2014).

2   Neil Postman, *The End of Education: Redefining the Value of School* (New York: Vintage, 1996).

3   Kenneth Strike, *Ethical Leadership in Schools: Creating Community in an Environment of Accountability* (New York: Corwin, 2006).

4   Carolyn Shields, *Transformative Leadership in Education: Equitable Change in an Uncertain and Complex World* (New York: Routledge, 2012).

5   http://innovationpartners.com

## Chapter One

1   Neil Postman, *The End of Education: Redefining the Value of School* (New York: Vintage, 1996).

2   Ibid.

3   Ibid.

4   Ibid.

5   Nancy Kober, "Why We Still Need Public Schools: Public Education for the Common Good" (Center on Education Policy Report, Washington, D.C.: 2007).

6   Ibid.

7   Ibid.

8   Ibid.

9   Fareed Zakaria, *In Defense of a Liberal Education*. (New York. W. W. Norton & Company, 2015).

10  Nancy Kober, "Why We Still Need Public Schools: Public Education for the Common Good" (Center on Education Policy Report, Washington, D.C.: 2007).

11  Ibid.

12　Ibid.

13　Ibid.

14　Ibid.

15　Ibid.

16　Ibid.

17　Ibid.

18　Ibid.

19　Michael Flanagan, "Final Speech to Michigan Educators" Michigan Department of Education, Spring 2015).

20　Leonard Burrello, Carl Lashley and Edith Beatty, *Educating All Students Together: How School Leaders Create Unified Systems* (Thousand Oaks, CA: Corwin, 2000).

21　Bill Gates, "Leaders Call for Equity, Rigor in the American High School" (Speech to National Governors Meeting, Washington, DC, 2005).

22　Michael Sandel, *Justice: What's the Right Thing to Do?* (New York: Farrar, Straus and Giroux, 2009).

23　David Cooperrider, "Positive Image, Positive Action: The Affirmative Basis of Organizing" in *Appreciative Inquiry: Rethinking Human Organization Toward a Positive Theory of Change*, ed. David Cooperrider, Peter Sorensen, Diane Whitney, and Therese Yaeger (Champaign, IL: Stipes Publishing, 1999).

24　Leonard C. Burrello, Lauren P. Hoffman, and Lynn E. Murray, *School Leaders Building Capacity from Within* (Thousand Oaks, CA: Corwin, 2005).

25　Ibid.

26　Ibid.

27　Ibid.

28　Ibid.

29　Michael Mantel and James Ludema, "Sustaining Positive Change: Inviting Conversational Convergence Through Appreciative Leadership and Organizational Design" in *Advances in Appreciative Inquiry*, eds. David Cooperrider and Michel Avital (UK: Emerald Group Publishing Limited, 2004), 209–336.

30　Leonard C. Burrello and Carmen Mills. (The Meridian Compass Report, 2014) Swift Center, University of Kansas.

31　Kenneth Strike, *Ethical Leadership in Schools: Creating Community in an Environment of Accountability* (New York: Corwin, 2006).

## Chapter Two

1　Frederic Laloux, *Reinventing Organizations*, (New York: Nelson-Parker, 2014), 13.

2　Ibid., 36.

3  Ibid., 56.

4  Ibid., 43–49.

5  Ibid., 56.

6  Ibid., 193.

7  Ibid., 39.

8  Ibid., 100.

9  Ibid., 101.

10 Frank Barrett, *Yes to the Mess: Surprising Leadership Lessons from Jazz* (Cambridge, MA: Harvard Business Review Press, 2012).

11 David Gershon, *Social Change 2.0: A Blueprint for Reinventing Our World* (Burlington, VT: High Point / Chelsea Green, 2009).

12 Robert Fritz, *The Path of Least Resistance: Learning to Become the Creative Force in Your Own Life* (New York: Ballantine Books, 1989).

13 David Gershon, *Social Change 2.0: A Blueprint for Reinventing Our World* (Burlington, VT: High Point / Chelsea Green, 2009).

14 Ibid.

15 Ibid.

16 Ibid.

17 Ibid.

18 Allen Moore, "Relational Leading, Neurons and Grandmothers" in *Brief Encounters from the Taos Institute* (Chagrin Falls, OH: Taos Institute, May 2015).

19 Kenneth Gergen, "Toward Generative Theory" in *Refiguring Self and Psychology* (Aldershot, England: Dartmouth Publishing Company, 1993).

20 Diana Whitney and Amanda Trosten-Bloom, *The Power of Appreciative Inquiry: A Practical Guide to Positive Change* (San Francisco: Berrett-Koehler, 2012).

21 Sarah Lewis, *Positive Psychology at Work: How Positive Leadership and Appreciative Inquiry Create Inspiring Organizations* (New York: Wiley-Blackwell, 2011).

22 David L. Cooperrider and Diana Whitney, *Appreciative Inquiry: A Positive Revolution in Change* (San Francisco: Berrett-Koehler Publishers, 2005).

23 Ibid.

24 James D. Ludema, Diana Whitney, Bernard Mohr, and Thomas J. Griffin, *The Appreciative Inquiry Summit: A Practitioner's Guide for Leading Large-Group Change* (San Francisco: Berrett-Koehler, 2003), 21.

25 Ibid., 21.

26 David Cooperrider, "Appreciative Inquiry in Organizational Life" in *Organizational Generativity: The Appreciative Inquiry Summit and a Scholarship of Transformation*, vol. 4 of *Advances in Appreciative Inquiry* (Bingley, England: Emerald Group Publishing, 2013), 36.

27 Gervase R. Bushe, "Generative Process, Generative Outcome: The Transformational Potential of Appreciative Inquiry" in *Organizational Generativity: The Appreciative Inquiry Summit and a Scholarship of Transformation*, vol. 4 of *Advances in Appreciative Inquiry* (Bingley, England: Emerald Publishing Group, 2013), 90.

28 Ibid.

29 Ibid.

30 Diane Whitney, "Designing Organizations as if Life Matters," in *Designing Information and Organizations with a Positive Lens*, vol. 2 of *Advances in Appreciative Inquiry* (Bingley, England: Emerald Group Publishing, 2008), 329–363.

31 Ibid.

32 Ibid.

33 Ibid.

34 Ibid.

35 Ibid.

36 Ibid.

37 Ibid.

38 Ibid.

39 Jane E. Dutton, Robert E. Quinn, and Kim S. Cameron, eds., *Positive Organizational Scholarship: Foundations of a New Discipline* (San Francisco: Berrett-Koehler, 2003).

40 Kim S. Cameron and Gretchen M. Spreitzer, eds., *The Oxford Handbook of Positive Organizational Scholarship* (Oxford: Oxford University Press, 2011).

41 Ibid., abstract.

42 Jacqueline M. Stavros, Gina Hinrichs and Sue Annis Hammond, *The Thin Book of SOAR: Building Strengths-Based Strategy* (Bend, OR: Thin Book Publishing, 2009), 11–12.

43 http://www.taosinstitute.net/healthy-kids-healthy-schools.

44 William Ury, *Getting to Yes with Yourself and Other Worthy Opponents* (New York: HarperCollins, 2015).

45 Ibid., 1.

46 Ibid., 176–177.

47 Bob Anderson, *Mastering Leadership* (Salt Lake City, UT: The Leadership Circle, 2012).

48 Michael Fullan, "Choosing the Wrong Drivers for Whole System Reform" (Centre for Strategic Education Seminar Series Paper No. 204, 2011).

49 Brené Brown, *Daring Greatly: How the Courage to be Vulnerable Transforms the Way We Live, Love, Parent, and Lead* (New York: Avery, 2015).

50 Michael Fullan, *Leadership and Sustainability: System Thinkers in Action* (New York: Corwin, 2004)

## Chapter Three

1  Keith Oatley and Maja Djikic, "How Reading Transforms Us," *New York Times*, SundayReview, 19 Dec. 2014, online.

2  Lone Hersted and Kenneth J. Gergen, *Relational Leading: Practices for Dialogically Based Collaboration* (Chagrin Falls, OH: Taos Institute, 2013), 30.

3  Ibid.

4  Carolyn M. Shields, "Dialogic Leadership for Social Justice: Overcoming Pathologies of Silence," *Educational Administration Quarterly* 40 (Feb 2004): 109.

5  Leslie Tucker, Roundstone International, roundstoneintl.com.

6  Diana Whitney, Amanda Trosten-Bloom, David Cooperrider, and Brian S. Kaplin, *Encyclopedia of Positive Questions* (New York: Crown Custom Publishing, 2014).

7  H. Peter Dachler and Dian-Marie Hosking, "The Primacy of Relations in Socially Constructing Organizational Realities" in *Management and Organization: Relational Perspectives*, eds Dian-Marie Hosking, Peter Dachler and Kenneth Gergen (Ashgate/Avebury, 1995), 3.

8  Ibid.

9  Ibid.

10  Barbara Fredrickson, *Positivity: Top-Notch Research Reveals the Upward Spiral that Will Change Your Life* (Easton, PA: Harmony Press, 2009), 123.

11  Jack Zenger, "One Secret for Greatness: Choose the Right Leadership Development Goals," *Forbes*, (May 2014), http://www.forbes.com/sites/jackzenger/2014/05/02/one-secret-for-greatness-choose-the-right-leadership-development-goals/.

12  Martin Seligman, *Flourish: A Visionary New Understanding of Happiness and Well-Being* (New York: Atria Books, 2012).

13  Diana Whitney, Amanda Trosten-Bloom, David Cooperrider, and Brian S. Kaplin, *Encyclopedia of Positive Questions* (New York: Crown Custom Publishing, 2014).

14  C. R. Snyder, *Handbook of Hope: Theory, Measures, and Applications* (New York: Academic Press, 2000).

15  Tony Alessandra, *The Official Site of Tony Alessandra*, 2015, http://www.alessandra.com/tahome.asp.

16  Denis Waitley, *Denis Waitley: Financial, Professional and Personal Success*, 2015, http://www.waitley.com/.

17  William Arthur Ward, *ReWard Yourself*, (Fort Worth Star-Telegraph, 1986).

18  Emily Hanford, "Grit, Luck and Money," American RadioWorks (American Public Media: Aug 2012).

19  Maria Popova, "Wanderlust: Rebecca Solnit on How Walking Vitalizes Meanderings of the Mind," *Brain Pickings* (2015).

## Chapter Four

1   Anthony Bryk et al, *Charting Chicago School Reform: Democratic Localism as a Lever for Change* (New York: Westview Press, 1999).

2   Kenneth J. Gergen, "Toward Generative Theory." *Journal of Personality and Social Psychology* 36, no. 11 (1978): 1,346.

3   Donald Schön, *The Reflective Practitioner: How Professionals Think in Action* (New York: Basic Books, 1984), 138.

4   Frank Barrett and David Cooperrider, "Generative Metaphor Intervention: A New Approach for Working with Systems Divided by Conflict and Caught in Defensive Perception," in *Appreciative Inquiry: An Emerging Direction for Organization Development* eds. David L. Cooperrider, Peter F. Sorensen, Therese F. Yaeger, and Diana Whitney (Champaign, IL: Stipes, 2001).

5   Ibid.

6   Peter Senge, *The Fifth Discipline: The Art & Practice of the Learning Organization* (New York: Doubleday, 2006).

7   Denise Caron, *It's a VUCA World*, online audio presentation, 4:45, March 5 2009, http://www.slideboom.com/presentations/72008/It's-a-VUCA-world---CIPS-CIO-March-5-2009.

8   Bill Jensen, secondary director of education, Columbus, IN, in discussion with the author, February 5, 2015.

9   Brian Binggeli, superintendent of schools, Plano, TX, in discussion with the author, November 12, 2014.

10  Ibid.

11  Matt Hill, superintendent of schools, Burbank, CA, in discussion with the author, March 2015.

12  Alvin Taylor, superintendent of schools, Meridian, MS, in discussion with the author, December 1, 2014.

13  Michael Riggle, superintendent of schools, Glenbrook, Illinois in discussion with the author, December 4, 2014.

14  David L. Cooperrider, Diana Whitney, and Jacqueline Stavros, *The Appreciative Inquiry Handbook: For Leaders of Change* (San Francisco: Berrett-Koehler, 2008).

15  Ibid.

16  Ibid.

17  Alvin Taylor, superintendent of schools, Meridian, MS, in discussion with the author, December 1, 2014.

18  David L. Cooperrider, Diana Whitney, and Jacqueline Stavros, *The Appreciative Inquiry Handbook: For Leaders of Change* (San Francisco: Berrett-Koehler, 2008).

19  Brian Binggeli, superintendent of schools, Plano, TX, in discussion with the author, November 12, 2014.

20 Frank J. Barrett and Ronald E. Fry, *Appreciative Inquiry: A Positive Approach to Building Cooperative Capacity* (Chagrin Falls, OH: Taos Institute Publishing, 2005).

21 Peter Senge, *The Fifth Discipline: The Art & Practice of the Learning Organization* (New York: Doubleday, 2006).

22 Frank J. Barrett and Ronald E. Fry, *Appreciative Inquiry: A Positive Approach to Building Cooperative Capacity* (Chagrin Falls, OH: Taos Institute Publishing, 2005).

23 Alvin Taylor, superintendent of schools, Meridian, MS, in discussion with the author, December 1, 2014.

24 Thomas J. Peters and Robert H. Waterman, Jr., *In Search of Excellence* (New York: Warner Books, 1982).

## Chapter Five

1 Richard Elmore, *Building a New Structure for School Leadership* (Washington, DC: Albert Shaker Institute, 2000).

2 Ibid.

3 Ibid.

4 Neil Postman, *The End of Education: Redefining the Value of School* (New York: Vintage, 1996).

5 Larry Cuban, "Redefining 'Good Schools' " (Teachers College lecture series at Columbia University, New York, New York, October 2001).

6 Ibid.

7 Martin E. P. Seligman, *Flourish: A Visionary New Understanding of Happiness and Well-Being* (New York: Atria Books, 2012).

8 Ibid.

9 Ibid.

10 Karin Chenoweth, *"It's Being Done": Academic Success in Unexpected Schools* (Cambridge, MA: Harvard Educational Publishing Group, 2007).

11 Ibid.

12 Alvin Taylor, superintendent of schools, Meridian, MS, in discussion with the author, December 1, 2014.

## Chapter Six

1 Wayne Sailor, Schoolwide Integrated Framework for Transformation (SWIFT) Center. University of Kansas.

2 Rebecca Holcombe, "Memorandum to Parents and Caregivers." Vermont Agency of Education. August 6, 2014.

3    Ibid.

4    Ibid.

5    William Foster, "Toward a Critical Practice of Leadership," In *Critical Perspectives on Educational Leadership* ed. J. Smyth, (London: Falmer Press, 1989).

6    Leonard C. Burrello, Lauren P. Hoffman, and E. Lynn Murray, *School Leaders Building Capacity from Within: Resolving Competing Agendas Creatively* (New York: Corwin, 2004).

7    Ibid.

8    Ibid.

9    Ibid.

## Afterword

1    Gallup, "State of America's Schools: The Path to Winning Again in Education" (2014).

2    Ibid.

3    Ibid.

4    Raju Mandhyan, "Stories as Drivers of Engagement and Innovation," *Insights* (March, 2015). http://www.rajumandhyan.com/2015/03/10/stories-as-drivers-of-engage-ment-and-innovation/.

## Narratives & Exercises

1    Martin Seligman, *Flourish: A Visionary New Understanding of Happiness and Well-Being* (New York: Atria, 2012), 89–90.

# ACKNOWLEDGMENTS

As you might expect, as our writing team came together, we grew in our respect for one another, finding collective inspiration from the work of the scholars in appreciative inquiry and many others in educational leadership circles. This collaboration ultimately led to our creating our own theory of action: the appreciative organizing graphic depicting the six spheres of influence interacting with one another that lead to positive narratives for public education.

We shared our first draft of the book early on with our colleagues Bruce Barnett from the University of Texas–San Antonio and Ronald Barnes, our referent superintendent who helped us better understand how both administrators in schools and those in training with university faculty might use our work. They told us the book was relevant and powerful and the exercises were important for coming to use Appreciative Inquiry and active implementation research. We also asked both Drs. Bill Miller, the executive director of the Michigan Intermediate School District Association, and Lynn Murray, a former Vermont principal now living in Oriental, North Carolina, to take a deep dive into the second version of the manuscript. They were superb editors who made the work more accessible and free of educational jargon.

This book could not have been written without the rich and deeply thoughtful conversations we had with superintendents and district leaders Brian Binggeli, Bill Jensen, George Van Horn, Linda DeClue, Michael Riggle, Dena Cushenberry, Alvin Taylor, Amy Carter, Robin Miles, Sonja Roberts, Roderick Jones, and Matt Hill. We thank the University of Kansas, SWIFT Center for their support of our work (especially Wayne Sailor, SWIFT Center Director, and Amy McCart, Director of Technical Assistance), and my SWIFT Center local partner, Karmen Mills.

As we plan the work that will grow of this book, we thank Edith Beatty of Vermont, Holly Heaviland of Michigan, and Megan Trierweiler of Tampa, who helped us guide our use of the book and its practices with district leadership and schools across the nation. The authors have also had the opportunity to use the book with our Gulf Coast Partnership training program, and with the Hillsborough County Wallace grant advanced principals training cohort. We thank them for their helpful feedback and engagement of our ideas and exercises.

Finally, this book's orientation, careful development, and close editing was supported by our publisher, Jotham Burrello, and his team at Elephant Rock Books, Fisheye Graphic Services, and Dena Cushenberry, Debbie Mann, Ramzi and Jana Beitz Nakhleh. This was truly a family affair.

# ABOUT THE AUTHORS

Leonard C. Burrello was a professor of educational leadership at the universities of Michigan, Indiana, and South Florida for forty-five years. Currently he's the executive director of the Center for Appreciative Organizing in Education. He's traveled domestically and internationally to study, document, and produce video exemplars of school districts, schools, and teaching and learning methods.

Linda M. Beitz has worked as a change agent with hundreds of people in school districts, nonprofits, state departments, court mediation programs, businesses, and communities. Over the years she has learned the change we seek in others begins with self-awareness and a commitment to communicating in ways that foster productive relationships.

John L. Mann was a principal, director of Leadership Development, and assistant superintendent in Pasco County, Florida, for twenty-eight years. After training administrators locally, nationally, and internationally, he now coordinates a principal preparation program focusing on Appreciative Inquiry and Organizing for the University of South Florida and several school districts.